# FEDERAL JURISDICTION

## IN A NUTSHELL

Fourth Edition

By

DAVID P. CURRIE
Edward H. Levi Distinguished Service Professor
The Law School
The University of Chicago

**WEST**
**GROUP**

ST. PAUL, MINN.
**1999**

TEXT IS PRINTED ON 10% POST CONSUMER RECYCLED PAPER

# PREFACE

The first edition of this Nutshell was derived from a series of lectures in which I attempted to summarize both the complex law governing the powers of the federal courts and my own opinions on the subject. The present edition brings these lectures up to date.

It is my hope that this volume may serve both to help students recapture the essence of the governing law and to stimulate thinking about the proper role of federal courts in our federal system.

# CONTENTS

# INTRODUCTION

As we know from the tenth amendment, the Federal Government has only those powers conferred on it by the Constitution. This is no less true of the federal courts; the judicial power of the United States is defined and limited by Article III.

The authority of the federal courts extends only to *judicial* matters; the subjects listed in Article III are all described as either "cases" or "controversies." Only certain categories of cases or controversies, moreover, are included – defined either by the nature of the underlying dispute or the identity of the parties. The limitations on federal jurisdiction thus reflect concerns both of federalism and of the separation of powers.

The most important types of cases and controversies that fall within federal judicial power are those arising under federal law (federal-question cases); those between citizens of different states or between citizens of a state and of a foreign country (diversity cases); those involving vessels on navigable waters (admiralty or maritime cases); those in which the United States is a party; and suits between states. Cases in this last category fall within the limited "original" (trial-court) jurisdiction of the Supreme Court, often involve such matters as boundary disputes or allocation of the waters of interstate streams, and are commonly farmed out to special masters for findings and recommendations.

Article III prescribes that the federal judicial power shall be vested "in one Supreme Court, and in such inferior courts as the Congress may from time to time ordain and establish." Pursuant to this provision, the Judiciary Act of 1789 not only established a Supreme Court to be composed of six Justices; it also created two sets of lower federal courts, the district courts and the circuit courts.

The district courts were exclusively courts of original jurisdiction. They served as trial courts principally in maritime cases and in the prosecution of minor federal crimes. There were thirteen districts, each with its own judge; the divisions were made essentially on state lines.

The districts were grouped into three circuits, each with a circuit court composed of two Supreme Court Justices and the local district judge. The circuit courts had both original and appellate functions. On the one hand, they reviewed decisions of the district courts; on the other, they were the trial courts for diversity cases and for major government litigation. Neither the district nor the circuit courts were given general jurisdiction over cases arising under federal law.

As Article III envisioned, the Supreme Court's jurisdiction was largely appellate: It was given power to review civil decisions of the circuit

courts and state-court decisions denying federal
rights.

In 1875 the district courts were given general
federal-question jurisdiction. In 1891, to allevi-
ate the increasing flood of cases, Congress created the circuit courts of appeals and for the first
time gave the Supreme Court control over its
docket by introducing the discretionary writ of
certiorari. In 1911 the old circuit courts, which
had been a burden on Supreme Court Justices,
were abolished.

The present jurisdictional statute (Title 28
U.S.C.) derives from a 1948 revision. Today the
district courts, at least one in every state, are the
principal federal trial courts. There are twelve
regional courts of appeals with power to review
most district-court decisions and many decisions of federal administrative agencies. The
Supreme Court's jurisdiction is principally appellate and principally discretionary. A specialized Court of Appeals for the Federal Circuit exercises appellate jurisdiction chiefly in patent
and government-contract cases. There are additional bodies sometimes known as legislative
courts, including territorial courts, the Tax
Court, and the Court of Appeals for the Armed
Forces.

Congress tinkers repeatedly with the jurisdictional provisions; the field is one of constant
change. Comprehensive proposals for revision of

the Judicial Code, however, have so far attracted little legislative support.

# I. CONGRESS, THE COURTS, AND THE CONSTITUTION

## A. JUDICIAL REVIEW

In the course of holding that it had no jurisdiction to issue an original writ of mandamus to a federal officer, the Supreme Court in *Marbury v. Madison*[1] concluded among other things that federal courts had the power and the duty to determine the constitutionality of acts of Congress. Chief Justice Marshall's opinion for the Court traced this authority to four constitutional sources.

Marshall described judicial review as inherent in written constitutions; yet the French constitution, adopted just a few years before, expressly forbade the judges to meddle with legislation. He relied also on Article III's provision extending the judicial power to constitutional cases, on Article VI's requirement that the judges swear to uphold the Constitution, and on the supremacy clause of the same Article, which makes only those laws enacted "pursuant to" the Constitution the supreme law of the land.

None of these provisions necessarily implies judicial review. The clause conferring jurisdiction over constitutional cases requires the judges to decide what the Constitution means; the oath

---

[1] 5 U.S. 137 (1803).

requires them to do what the Constitution
commands. If the Constitution does not provide
for judicial review, a refusal to determine the
validity of federal statutes conforms with both
provisions. The supremacy clause, in turn,
speaks of laws enacted pursuant to *this* Constitution"; the following words according
supremacy to "treaties *made, or which shall be
made*, under the authority of the United States"
suggest that the purpose was not to distinguish
valid from invalid laws but to deny supremacy to
those made under our earlier constitution, the
Articles of Confederation.

This is not to say that Marshall's conclusion
was wrong. At the time of the Constitutional
Convention there were precedents for judicial
review of municipal, colonial, and state legislation, by analogy to the familiar *ultra vires* doctrine in corporate law. The Convention records,
moreover, confirm a widespread expectation that
the courts would review the constitutionality of
federal laws. In arguing against the creation of
a Council of Revision to review federal statutes,
for example, Rufus King of Massachusetts
insisted that "the Judges will have the
expounding of those laws when they come before
them; and they will no doubt stop the operation of
such as shall appear repugnant to the
Constitution." James Madison said much the
same thing in the House of Representatives in
proposing the Bill of Rights in 1789.

Judicial review is thus firmly established, and the argument for its legitimacy is strong. Yet there remains a crucial ambiguity in the *Marbury* opinion, and this ambiguity is highly relevant to a number of important questions considered in this book. At one point Marshall appears to treat judicial review as a mere byproduct of the traditional judicial function of deciding cases. In order to decide a case, said Marshall, a court must determine what the law is; if a statute conflicts with the Constitution it is not the law, as the latter is supreme. Elsewhere in the same opinion, however, Marshall treats judicial review as an indispensable element in the constitutional scheme of checks and balances. Express limitations on legislative authority, he argued, would be worthless if the courts were required to enforce unconstitutional laws: "It would be giving to the legislature a practical and real omnipotence, with the same breath which professes to restrict their powers within narrow limits. It is prescribing limits, and declaring that those limits may be passed at pleasure." Alexander Hamilton had said the same thing in the Federalist: "The courts were designed to be an intermediate body between the people and the legislature, in order . . . to keep the latter within the limits assigned to their authority."

If judicial review represents nothing more than a sort of clean-hands doctrine for judges – a requirement that the judges themselves not violate the Constitution – then there is no cause for concern if Congress strips the Supreme Court of jurisdiction to decide constitutional cases, packs it with additional Justices of its own persuasion, or – as it did in 1802 – rearranges the Court's terms so that for fourteen months it will not sit at all. If judicial review is an essential part of the Framers' plan to keep other branches from exceeding their powers, however, any such measure poses a grave threat to the Constitution itself.


## B. CASES AND CONTROVERSIES

Article III extends the judicial power to "cases" and "controversies" of specified types, and the Supreme Court has made clear that matters not qualifying as judicial "cases" or "controversies" cannot be entrusted to courts created under Article III. This principle embraces a number of different limitations on the authority of the courts.


### 1. Finality

The courts will not act if their decisions are subject to executive or legislative review. This principle was established in 1792 in *Hayburn's Case*,[2] in which five Justices sitting on circuit refused to pass upon veterans' pension claims

---

[2] 2 U.S. 408.

because the statute allowed the Secretary of War to disregard their findings if he discovered imposition or mistake. This limitation seems a rather obvious corollary of Article III's guarantees of tenure during good behavior and irreducible salary. If, as Hamilton said in the Federalist Papers, the reason for these provisions is to insulate the process of decision from executive or legislative influence, executive power to set aside a judicial decision is intolerable.

Nevertheless the finality of judicial decisions is a question of degree. Congress can frustrate a money judgment against the United States by refusing to appropriate money to pay it, and any other federal judgment can be defeated if the executive fails to call out the troops to enforce it. It is probably for this reason that Professor Bickel termed finality the least important element of the case-or-controversy requirement.

## 2. Advisory Opinions

In Massachusetts and in Canada the courts will give advice to the executive or to the legislature on important public questions. The federal courts in this country will not. In 1793, at President Washington's request, Secretary of State Jefferson asked the Justices their opinions on a number of abstract legal questions respecting American neutrality in the war then raging between England and France. In a cryptic letter to

Jefferson the Justices declined to answer the President's questions.

There is something to be said for the practice of giving advisory opinions. It avoids the delays and uncertainties of ordinary litigation, and it facilitates judicial review. But advisory opinions have disadvantages as well. Concrete facts help the court to understand the full import of its decision; adverse parties help to ensure that both sides of the question will be adequately presented. Abstract pronouncements on questions of law may bring the courts into unnecessary conflict with other branches of government; judicial lawmaking is least difficult to reconcile with democracy when it is the inevitable byproduct of the stock business of deciding individual disputes; the time spent in resolving abstract questions may distract the judges from their more central function. The modern explanation for the Supreme Court's position is that a request for an advisory opinion does not present a case or controversy within the meaning of Article III.

Related to the question of what functions the courts may perform is the question whether judges may be asked to step off the Bench to perform nonjudicial duties. Two early Chief Justices were sent off to negotiate treaties with foreign nations; Justice Robert Jackson took a year off to prosecute war criminals at Nuremberg; Chief Justice Warren investigated the assassination of President Kennedy.

There are at least three kinds of objections to this sort of activity: the loss of time that could otherwise be devoted to judicial tasks, the risk of controversy that might impair public confidence in judicial decisions, and the danger that judges might be tempted to render decisions that will please the executive in order to attract desirable appointments. Nevertheless, in *Mistretta v. United States*[3] the Court held that federal judges could constitutionally sit on a commission to draft sentencing guidelines for criminal cases. History showed, the Court said, that the Constitution "does not forbid judges from wearing two hats; it merely forbids them from wearing both hats at the same time."

### 3. Standing

"The Article III judicial power," said the Supreme Court in *Warth v. Seldin* in 1975,[4] "exists only to redress or otherwise to protect against injury to the complaining party." A litigant who does not "stand to profit in some personal interest" by prevailing on his claim, as the Court said in *Simon v. Eastern Ky. Welfare Rights Org.* the following year,[5] has not presented a case or controversy; he is said to lack standing to challenge the validity of government action.

---

[3]487 U.S. 1231 (1988).
[4]422 U.S. 490.
[5]426 U.S. 26 (1976).

The same minimum requirement of injury is found in numerous statutes conferring the right to challenge federal administrative action. The Administrative Procedure Act (APA), for example, authorizes judicial review at the behest of a person "adversely affected or aggrieved by agency action within the meaning of a relevant statute . . . ."[6]

Standing in this sense is not an artificial limitation designed to restrict constitutional litigation. In private law I cannot sue for a trespass on my neighbor's land. In terms of the policies that underlie the case-or-controversy requirement, as the Court said in *Baker v. Carr*,[7] a litigant needs a "personal stake in the outcome" in order to "assure that concrete adverseness which sharpens the presentation of issues . . . ."

It is not always easy to determine what constitutes an adequate injury to support standing under the Constitution or the APA. In language equally applicable to the constitutional question, the Court held in *Sierra Club v. Morton*[8] that a mere "value preference" or "intellectual interest in the problem" of conservation did not suffice under the statute: The Club could not challenge the development of a ski resort on wilderness land without alleging that its members were

---

[6]5 U.S.C. § 702.
[7]369 U.S. 186 (1962).
[8]405 U.S. 727 (1972).

users of the area. On the other hand, in *United States v. SCRAP*[9] the Court allowed park users to attack a rate decision of the Interstate Commerce Commission on the basis of allegations that it would discourage transportation of recycled materials and thus damage the parks through extraction of raw materials and disposal of refuse. It was no ground for objection, the Court said, that the alleged injury was esthetic rather than economic, that it might not be substantial, or that it was shared by many other people.

In the *Simon* case, quoted above, the Court refused to allow indigents to attack the charitable tax exemption of hospitals that refused them free services, finding their allegation that invalidation of the exemption would induce the hospitals to serve them too speculative to support constitutional standing. In *Warth v. Seldin*, moreover, the Court imposed a strict pleading requirement that seems difficult to reconcile with earlier interpretations of the Federal Rules of Civil Procedure. It was not enough, the Court said, to allege generally that restrictive zoning ordinances had prevented prospective builders from constructing low-cost housing and prospective tenants from moving into the city; the latter had to "allege facts from which it reasonably could be inferred that, absent the respondents' restrictive zoning practices, there is a substantial probability that they would have been able to

---

[9]412 U.S. 669 (1973).

purchase or lease," and the former that they had a "special project . . . that is currently precluded . . . by the ordinance. . . ." Three years later, however, in *Duke Power Co. v. Carolina Envir. Study Group, Inc.*,[10] the Court found adequate proof of injury when plaintiffs complained that a proposed nuclear power plant would expose them to radiation, and that the plant would not be constructed in the absence of a challenged limitation of liability in case of accident.

The Court's insistence that injury is a constitutional requirement means that Congress cannot confer standing on a person with nothing to gain by suing.[11] Conversely, it seems clear that Congress may constitutionally confer standing on anyone injured by the action she attacks. In *FCC v. Sanders Bros. Radio Station*,[12] for example, the Supreme Court upheld the right of a broadcast licensee to attack the grant of a license to a competitor under a statute authorizing suit by persons "aggrieved" or "adversely affected," even though in the absence of statute the Court had held that in similar situations a competitor could not sue.

Apart from the constitutional question of case or controversy, as the Court said in *Warth v. Seldin*, the question whether a plaintiff has

---

[10]438 U.S. 59 (1978).
[11]Lujan v. Defenders of Wildlife, 504 U.S. 555 (1992); Eaines v. Byrd, 521 U.S. 811 (1997).
[12]309 U.S. 470 (1940).

standing is essentially whether the law gives him an explicit or implicit right of action. Sometimes, as in the *Sanders* case, a statute clearly authorizes suit by anyone who is injured in the constitutional sense. In other cases the Court has held that a substantive statutory or constitutional provision impliedly creates a right of action for an injured member of the class the provision was designed to protect. Thus the Court has allowed damage actions by investors harmed by violations of the fraud provisions of the securities laws[13] and by victims of unreasonable searches or seizures.[14] Similarly, in 1968 the Court upheld the standing of a power company to enforce a geographical limitation on the TVA's authority to sell electricity on the ground that the purpose of the limitation was to protect other companies from TVA competition.[15] Indeed in the important case of *Association of Data Processing Service Organizations v. Camp*[16] the Court generalized the principle of these decisions by construing the Administrative Procedure Act, which as noted authorizes judicial review at the behest of anyone "adversely affected or aggrieved by agency action within the meaning of a relevant statute," to confer standing upon any injured person "arguably within the zone of

---

[13]J. I. Case Co. v. Borak, 377 U.S. 426 (1964).

[14]Bivens v. Six Unknown Named Agents, 403 U.S. 388 (1971).

[15]Hardin v. Kentucky Utils. Co., 390 U.S. 1.

[16]397 U.S. 150 (1970).

interests to be protected or regulated by the statute or constitutional guarantee in question."

There are private-law analogies to these decisions. The first Restatement of Torts, for example, laid down the principle that one might sue for injuries caused by violation of a criminal statute if the injury was one the statute was meant to prevent. Yet the Supreme Court has been increasingly reluctant to infer private damage remedies from a silent statute,[17] and occasional separate opinions have gone so far as to suggest that the Court has no business creating rights of action at all.

In light of the Rules of Decision Act (28 U.S.C. § 1652) and the decision in *Erie R.R. v. Tompkins*,[18] which severely limit the federal common law, this position has considerable force. Moreover, since the 1948 extension of the Rules of Decision Act to equity cases and the repeal of the Conformity Act provision (1 Stat. 93) on which the power to create judicial remedies in equity was based, the same objection can plausibly be raised against inferring standing in equity from a statute that does not speak to the subject. As for the Administrative Procedure Act, the time may be ripe for a return to the original understanding that the reference to persons "adversely affected or aggrieved . . . within the

---

[17]E.g., Transamerica Mortgage Advisors, Inc. v. Lewis, 444 U.S. 11 (1979).
[18]304 U.S. 64 (1938).

meaning of a relevant statute" confers no standing in itself but merely recognizes that other statutes, like the one in *Sanders*, may confer standing on persons "adversely affected or aggrieved."[19]

Frequently, however, despite the statement in *Warth* that the nonconstitutional question of standing is whether the plaintiff has a judicial remedy, the Court has treated standing as if it were an entirely separate issue. Thus in the *Duke Power* case noted above, after finding a constitutionally sufficient injury, the Court declared that there were "other limits" on standing derived from "general prudential concerns" about the proper role of the courts. Specifically, the opinion continued – relying on similar language from *Warth v. Seldin* – one did not generally have standing to litigate "a generalized grievance shared by a large number of citizens in a substantially equal measure" or "to assert the legal rights of another."

As an example of a "generalized grievance" the Court cited *United States v. Richardson*,[20] where a citizen argued for more complete accounting of appropriations to the Central Intelligence Agency under Article I, § 9. It may well be that this provision was not designed to confer enforceable rights on individual citizens, though

---

[19]Kansas City Power & Light Co. v. McKay, 225 F.2d 924 (D.C. Cir. 1955).
[20]418 U.S. 166 (1974).

the arguably analogous Freedom of Information
Act does. It hardly seems an appropriate reason
for denying relief, however, that the Government
has harmed many citizens rather than only a
few.

The principle that one cannot generally assert
the rights of others, also noted in *Duke Power*, is
of long standing. It embraces, however, two
distinct propositions. In *McGowan v.
Maryland*,[21] for example, the Court held that store
employees who were not themselves Sabbatarians could not defend a prosecution for selling goods on Sunday by arguing that the statute
could not constitutionally be applied to those who
celebrated the Sabbath on another day. This decision was an elementary application of the case-
or-controversy requirement. For normal
severability principles meant that the complaining employees could be prosecuted even if
Sabbatarians could not; they had nothing to gain
by asserting the rights of others.

*Tileston v. Ullman*,[22] however, was another
story. In that case a doctor was not permitted to
argue that for the State to forbid *him* to give birth-
control information infringed the constitutional
rights of his patients. There was no doubt that the
doctor had suffered a constitutionally sufficient
injury; unlike the complainants in *McGowan*,

---

[21]366 U.S. 420 (1961).
[22]318 U.S. 44 (1943).

he foundered on a *prudential* limitation on standing.

The principle that one may not assert third-party rights is easy enough to state, but it is not always easy to determine whether the complainant is asserting only the rights of others. It was arguable, for example, that the doctor in *Tileston* had a constitutional right of his own to prescribe birth control for his patients. The analysis of the purposes of the relevant substantive provisions practiced in such cases as *Data Processing* may be helpful in answering this threshold question.

The lessons of *Data Processing*, however, seem to have been overlooked in *Duke Power*, where the Court upheld the standing of persons injured by the radiation from normal operation of a power plant to challenge a limitation on liability for catastrophic nuclear accidents. Presumably the persons protected by the asserted requirement of full compensation for such accidents were the accident victims themselves, yet the Court held without discussion that the plaintiffs were asserting their own rights and not those of third parties.

Later opinions have occasionally listed *Data Processing*'s "zone of interests" test as an additional "prudential" limitation on standing in general, although it was initially intended as an interpretation of the APA. This addition may turn out to be largely redundant, as the zone test is a common method of determining whether or not a litigant is asserting her own rights.

Finally, the prudential restriction on asserting third-party rights is by no means absolute. In *Barrows v. Jackson*[23] and in *NAACP v. Alabama*[24] the Supreme Court allowed parties to invoke the rights of others because they were not in a position to assert them for themselves. *Craig v. Boren*[25] arguably carried this exception beyond its justification, allowing a beer vendor to argue that her potential male customers were victims of sex discrimination, though the dissent found no barrier to an action by the customers themselves.

The most striking feature of the *Duke Power* opinion, however, is that it upheld the plaintiffs' right to sue without identifying what law gave them the right to do so. That there are no prudential objections to the exercise of authority should not be enough to justify the suit; as the Court said in *Warth v. Seldin*, there must be an explicit or implicit right of action. Perhaps the Court meant to say that, absent statutory restrictions, everyone has a federal common-law right to challenge any governmental action that adversely affects him in the exercise of his own non-generalized rights. If so, it ought to have

---

[23]346 U.S. 249 (1953).
[24]357 U.S. 449 (1958).
[25]429 U.S. 190 (1976).

explained how the existence of this common law was consistent with *Erie R.R. v. Tompkins*.

Cases involving the standing of taxpayers deserve special mention. In *Frothingham v. Mellon*[26] the Supreme Court held a federal taxpayer could not challenge an expenditure to promote maternal health because her interest was too small, because it was shared by too many other people, and because it was not clear that a victory would in fact reduce her tax bill. Yet in *Flast v. Cohen*[27] the Court allowed a federal taxpayer to challenge federal grants to church schools as an establishment of religion. Two requirements, the Court said, had to be met and were met in *Flast*: The taxpayer must be attacking "exercises of congressional power under the taxing and spending clause" rather than "an incidental expenditure of tax funds in the administration of an essentially regulatory statute"; and he must argue that the expenditure "exceeds specific constitutional limitations imposed upon the exercise of the congressional taxing and spending power," not simply that it is "beyond the powers delegated to Congress."

These two requirements were plucked out of thin air without precedent or explanation. Neither has any application outside the field of taxpayer suits, and neither has anything to do with

---

[26]262 U.S. 447 (1923).
[27]392 U.S. 83 (1968).

the extent of the plaintiff's stake in the outcome or with the likelihood that he will litigate aggressively. All the concerns that the Court had invoked in denying standing in *Frothingham* were present in *Flast*, yet the Court made no effort to answer the crucial argument that the taxpayer could not demonstrate injury, which it had elsewhere insisted was the constitutional minimum.

In distinguishing *Frothingham*, however, and in responding to Justice Harlan's dissenting observation that the Establishment Clause did not specifically limit expenditures, the Court suggested a line of argument that might suffice to bring *Flast* within the *Data Processing* test for standing. Mrs. Frothingham, said the Court in *Flast*, had attempted to assert the state's interest in a constitutional allocation of government power. One of the recognized purposes of the establishment clause, in contrast, was to protect taxpayers from having to support religion. In traditional terms, therefore, Frothingham was asserting the state's rights; Flast was asserting his own.

This analysis also helps to avoid the Court's conclusion in *Frothingham* that the possibility of a smaller tax bill was too speculative to provide a constitutionally cognizable injury. For even if a decision in Flast's favor would not put money in his pocket it would prevent a distinct constitutional injury: the use of his money, without his consent, to support religion.

A restrictive decision like *Frothingham* has a profound effect on the institution of judicial review, for it means that in most cases *nobody* is in a position to challenge federal expenditures. If, as Marshall said in one part of the *Marbury* opinion, judicial review is simply an incident to deciding cases, that is no cause for concern. If there is no case to decide, the judges cannot get their hands dirty, and there is no problem. But *Marbury* also stressed the importance of judicial review as a means of preventing Congress from overstepping its constitutional bounds. On this view, far from being compelled by the separation-of-powers doctrine as the Court supposed, the *Frothingham* decision impaired the system of checks and balances by enabling Congress to make unconstitutional expenditures with impunity.

### 4. Ripeness

A further element of the "case" or "controversy" requirement is that the matter must be "ripe" for decision.

The problem of ripeness is essentially one of prematurity. Often concrete facts are missing which would guide the Court in making a well-informed decision. Because it is not certain what is going to happen, or even whether anything is going to happen, the decision of an unripe case may be a waste of the court's time. It may result in unnecessary confrontation with another

branch of government, and, because it is not
certain that the parties have anything at stake, it
is not certain that the case will be adequately
argued. The question of ripeness often tends to
merge with that of standing: The plaintiffs have
not yet shown that they are the right parties to
make the asserted claim.

There was a time when the Supreme Court's
understandable reluctance to decide hypothetical
cases was pushed to the point of causing serious
hardship. In *United Public Workers v.
Mitchell*[28] the Court refused to allow government
employees to attack the validity of the Hatch Act,
which restricted their political activities, because
the precise nature of their intended political
activity was unclear and there was "no threat" of
interference with their activities "beyond that
implied by the existence of the law and the regulations." In *International Longshoremen's
Union v. Boyd*[29] resident aliens intending to do
summer work in Alaska were precluded from
challenging the government's decision to subject
them to the stringent requirements for new
entrants upon their return. In *Poe v. Ullman*[30]
the Court disallowed an attack on a Connecticut
birth-control statute on the ground that past
prosecutorial inertia demonstrated there was no
substantial threat that the law would be enforced.

---

[28]330 U.S. 75 (1947).
[29]347 U.S. 222 (1954).
[30]367 U.S. 497 (1961).

What the Court seemed to be saying in these cases was that the only way a person could test the validity of a statute was to violate it and incur the risk of punishment in case the court rejected his claim. As Professor Borchard said in criticizing comparable decisions, in effect the Court was telling the citizen that "the only way to determine whether the suspect is a mushroom or a toadstool is to eat it." It was precisely this kind of risk that the Declaratory Judgments Act was meant to avoid.

Even in older decisions, however, the Court did not always require that a litigant violate the law in order to test it. For example, in *Village of Euclid v. Ambler Realty Co.*[31] a property owner was permitted to attack the validity of a zoning ordinance without violating it because the mere existence of the ordinance reduced the value of its property. In *Adler v. Board of Education*[32] a teacher was allowed to challenge the validity of a law requiring dismissal of teachers who advocated the overthrow of the government although he did not allege that he had done or intended to do what the statute forbade. And in the *Railroad Transfer* case,[33] which seems to have gone too far, the plaintiff was permitted to attack a provision of a Chicago ordinance requiring the company to keep its principal place of business

---

[31]272 U.S. 365 (1926).

[32]342 U.S. 485 (1952).

[33]Railroad Transfer Service, Inc. v. City of Chicago, 386 U.S. 352 (1967).

within the city, even though there was no allegation that the company contemplated changing its place of business.

In recent years the Court has explicitly recognized that the risk of enforcement of a provision of debatable validity may place affected persons in a dilemma sufficiently constraining to create a ripe controversy. Thus in *Roe v. Wade*[34] a pregnant woman was allowed to attack a statute forbidding her to obtain an abortion; in *Abbott Laboratories v. Gardner*[35] a drug manufacturer was permitted to challenge a labeling requirement that had not yet been enforced.

But the Court has been careful to open the door only to cases it considers to present true hardships, and it is by no means easy to predict where the line between real and speculative controversies will be drawn. In a companion case to *Abbott*, for example, the Court held unripe a challenge to a regulation that it read as imposing "no irremediable adverse consequences" in the event of a later dispute.[36] The lower courts, following this lead, have properly refused to determine the validity of regulations that have merely been proposed and not adopted.[37] And in *Roe* itself the Court dismissed as "speculative" the challenge of a nonpregnant woman who al-

---

[34]410 U.S. 113 (1973).
[35]387 U.S. 136 (1967).
[36]Toilet Goods Ass'n v. Gardner, 397 U.S. 158 (1967).
[37]E.g., Lever Bros. v. FTC, 325 F. Supp. 371 (D.Me. 1971).

leged that uncertainty as to her ability to obtain an abortion interfered with her marriage.

As Professor Fritz Scharpf pointed out some years ago, the degree of ripeness required for an informed decision may be related to one's views on the merits of the case. In *Adler*, for example, a judge who believed that the state could never condition employment on the surrender of constitutional rights would need a less complete record than Justice Frankfurter, who thought the validity of the statute's application depended upon what the individual teacher might actually say.

The ripeness doctrine is related to the equitable considerations of irreparable harm that inform the traditional decision whether or not a case is appropriate for an injunction. It is also related to the notion that declaratory relief is discretionary, and to the principle requiring exhaustion of administrative remedies. Like the doctrine of standing, it has both constitutional and prudential dimensions.

## 5. Mootness

In moot cases the facts have already happened, so that there is no problem of lack of concreteness. But the case no longer matters to the parties, and therefore the decision of such a case would be a waste of time, might entail unnecessary conflict with other branches, and might very well be made without the benefit of proper adverse arguments. Unlike most jurisdictional questions, the issue of mootness often arises after a suit is filed, and a case will be dismissed or vacated if it becomes moot at any time before final appellate decision.

The problem of course is to decide when a case is moot and when it is not. In *Carafas v. LaVallee*,[38] for example, the Court held that the continuing disabilities attached by law to an ex-felon were sufficient to keep a controversy over his conviction alive even after his release from prison. In *United States v. W.T. Grant Co.*[39] the Court stated an important limitation: A case does not become moot simply because the challenged behavior has ceased if there is a substantial likelihood that it will be resumed.

In the past few decades the Supreme Court has created a novel exception to the ordinary mootness doctrine. In *Roe v. Wade*,[40] for example, a plaintiff seeking a declaration of her right to an abortion had been pregnant when she filed suit but was no longer so when the case reached the Supreme Court. To hold the case moot, the Court said, would effectively prevent judicial review of abortion questions because of the inevitably short period between conception and

---

[38]391 U.S. 234 (1968).
[39]345 U.S. 629 (1953).
[40]410 U.S. 113 (1973).

birth; the issue was "capable of repetition, yet evading review."

In a case in which time constraints otherwise would effectively insulate a law from judicial scrutiny, the Court's policy has its appeal; but it is difficult to see how the unavailability of normal review makes the matter any the less moot, or any more a constitutional "controversy." Moreover, *Roe* was a less than obvious case in which to apply the "evading review" exception, for in the same opinion the Court held a doctor had standing to challenge the abortion law, and there was no suggestion that his case was about to become moot.

In class actions the mootness doctrine has been even further eroded. The "evading review" exception was applied to a class action in *Sosna v. Iowa*[41] to allow a challenge to a residency requirement the representative plaintiff had satisfied during litigation. In *Franks v. Bowman Transp. Co.*[42] the Court unjustifiably relied on *Sosna* in holding that a plaintiff could continue to represent a class to which he no longer belonged even if the issue was not one that otherwise would evade review.

Initially the Court limited the authority of the mooted representative to cases in which the class

---

[41]410 U.S. 113 (1973).
[42]24 U.S. 747 (1976).

had been certified by the trial court.[43] In two 1980 decisions, however, the Court allowed plaintiffs to appeal from the refusal to certify a class although their own claims had been mooted.[44] In the latter case the named plaintiffs had been offered the full amount of their individual claims in settlement. The Court said they retained an interest "in their desire to shift part of the costs of litigation to those who will share in its benefits if the class is certified." The next step, which one hopes the Court will not take, is to hold that the same prospect of attorneys' fees gives a person standing to bring an action on behalf of a class of which he has never been a member.

## 6. Political Questions

In *Luther v. Borden*[45] the Supreme Court refused to determine which of two competing bodies was the legitimate government of Rhode Island. In *Pacific States Tel. Co. v. Oregon*[46] it refused to decide whether a state might constitutionally adopt legislation by initiative or referendum. In *Colegrove v. Green*[47] it refused to determine the constitutionality of an unequal apportionment of congressional seats. The reason given by the

---

[43]Indianapolis School Comm'rs v. Jacobs, 420 U.S. 128 (1975).

[44]United States Parole Comm. v. Geraghty, 445 U.S. 388; Deposit Guaranty Nat'l Bank v. Roper, 445 U.S. 326.

[45]48 U.S. 1 (1849).

[46]223 U.S. 118 (1912).

[47]328 U.S. 549 (1946).

Court in the first two cases, and by the famous opinion of Justice Frankfurter for three of the seven participating Justices in *Colegrove*, was that the issues were "political," not judicial.

The all-important decision in this area is *Baker v. Carr*,[48] in which the Court upheld a federal court's authority to determine the constitutionality of electoral districts for state legislators. The political-question doctrine, wrote Justice Brennan for the Court, was based upon "the relationship between the judiciary and coordinate branches of the Federal Government, and not the federal judiciary's relationship to the States."

> Prominent on the surface of any case held to involve a political question is found a textually demonstrable constitutional commitment of the issue to a coordinate political department; or a lack of judicially discoverable and manageable standards for resolving it; or the impossibility of deciding without an initial policy determination of a kind clearly for nonjudicial discretion; or the impossibility of a court's undertaking independent resolution without expressing lack of the respect due coordinate branches of government; or an unusual need for unquestioning adherence to a political decision already made; or the potentiality of embarrassment from multifarious pronouncements by various departments on one question . . . .

---

[48]369 U.S. 186 (1962).

None of these characteristics, the Court said, was present in *Baker v. Carr*.

The political-question doctrine was further eroded in *Powell v. McCormack*,[49] in which the Court upheld judicial authority to pass upon the exclusion of an elected Congressman from the House. The Article I provision making each House "Judge of the . . . Qualifications of its own Members," the Court ruled, "committed" to Congress at most the power to determine whether the constitutional requirements of age, citizenship, and residence were met, not to deny membership for alleged misuse of House funds. Two of the *Baker* criteria were given exceedingly short shrift: Deciding Powell's case would demonstrate no "lack of respect" for other branches, since it required only the traditional judicial exercise of interpreting the Constitution; nor would it result in "multifarious pronouncements . . . on one question," since the Court's word was law.

Yet the political-question doctrine began something of a comeback in several more recent decisions. Strictly speaking, *O'Brien v. Brown*[50] merely stayed enforcement of a lower-court decision respecting the seating of delegates to the 1972 Democratic National Convention. In weighing the public-interest and probability-of-success

---

[49]395 U.S. 486 (1969).
[50]409 U.S. 1 (1972).

criteria relevant to the stay question, however, the Court strongly suggested the ultimate issue was "political." In *Gilligan v. Morgan*[51] a bare majority in refusing to entertain an action to reform Ohio National Guard procedures after the shooting of student protesters at Kent State University invoked the political-question principle as well as other aspects of the case-or-controversy requirement. In *Goldwater v. Carter*[52] four Justices argued that the question whether the President could terminate a treaty was "political," essentially because the text of the Constitution did not answer the question and the subject was foreign affairs.

Most recently, in *Nixon v. United States*,[53] the Supreme Court refused to review the Senate's decision to appoint a committee to hear evidence in a proceeding to remove a federal judge. By giving the Senate "sole power" to try impeachments, Chief Justice Rehnquist wrote, Article I had excluded the courts not only from trying impeachments themselves but also from reviewing Senate decisions in such cases. This conclusion was no surprise; impeachment matters had long been cited as textbook examples of matters committed not to the discretion but to the final decision of someone other than the courts.

---

[51]413 U.S. 1 (1973).
[52]444 U.S. 996 (1979).
[53]506 U.S. 224 (1993).

Less convincingly, the Court added that Article I provided no justiciable standards for determining whether the Senate itself was required to hear evidence in an impeachment case. Justice White seemed quite right in protesting that the purpose of the "sole power" clause was to keep impeachment trials out of the courts, not to prescribe how evidence should be taken in the Senate.

In any event, whether or not there are adequate standards to permit effective judicial review depends in large part on one's view of the merits. There is no lack of standards for reapportionment, for example, if one agrees with the Court that the Constitution basically mandates numerical equality among districts. It is more difficult to find standards if one thinks, as Justice Frankfurter did, that the apportionment process must take account of a great many complicated demographic and geographical factors.

The tension between the political-question theory and the perception of courts as guardians of the Constitution is evident: Except where the designation reflects a decision that the Constitution commits the matter to the discretion of another branch, to characterize an issue as political means that the executive or the legislature may violate the Constitution and get away with it. Indeed, the argument that judicial review is indispensable to enforcement of the Constitution was made with especial force in regard to legislative apportionment, an area generally thought "political" before *Baker v. Carr*: The political processes for correcting intolerable legislation were not fully open, because in states lacking machinery to bypass the legislature in amending their constitutions political reform would have required legislators to surrender their own power.

## 7. Administrative Questions

In *Federal Radio Comm. v. General Electric Co.*[54] the Supreme Court held a federal court could not constitutionally be empowered to make a de novo determination of public convenience and necessity in the grant of a broadcasting license because the question was administrative rather than judicial. In the later *Nelson* case[55] the Court upheld a narrower review power over the same orders limited to questions of law and to the substantiality of the evidence.

Professors Hart and Wechsler suggested that the difficulty in *Federal Radio* was that the discretion conferred on the Court was too broad. A comparison with some admittedly judicial questions, however, shows that courts may be given a great deal of discretion – as in nuisance cases, in antitrust cases governed by the rule of reason,

---

[54]281 U.S. 464 (1930).
[55]Federal Radio Comm. v. Nelson Bros. B. & M. Co., 289 U.S. 266 (1933).

and in cases involving allegedly unreasonable searches. The principle of *Federal Radio* may have been significantly narrowed by the *Steelworkers* case,[56] which upheld judicial power to determine whether or not there was a national emergency justifying a strike injunction under the Taft-Hartley Act, and by the *City Bank* case,[57] in which the Supreme Court held it proper for a court to determine de novo whether community convenience justified an anti-competitive merger. Yet there may still be limits to the ability of Congress to entrust the courts with the making of open-ended policy decisions, even when there are concrete facts and adverse parties.

## C. THE POWER OF CONGRESS TO REGULATE FEDERAL JURISDICTION

### 1. The Power to Deny Jurisdiction

In 1964 Representative Tuck of Virginia introduced a bill that would have taken away the jurisdiction of both the district courts and the Supreme Court in reapportionment cases. Six years earlier, Senator Jenner's bill would have deprived the Supreme Court of jurisdiction over bar admissions, state subversion laws, congres-

---

[56]United Steelworkers v. United States, 361 U.S. 39 (1959).
[57]United States v. First City Nat'l Bank, 386 U.S. 361 (1967).

sional-committee cases, and cases arising out of the Federal Loyalty-Security Program.

A superficial glance at Article III may suggest that these bills would have been unconstitutional. For that Article provides that the judicial power of the United States "shall extend to all cases . . . arising under this Constitution" and that it "shall be vested" in certain federal courts.

Yet Article III also authorizes Congress to make "exceptions" to the appellate jurisdiction of the Supreme Court, and it contains no explicit requirement that there be inferior federal courts at all: The judicial power is vested in the Supreme Court and in "such inferior Courts as the Congress may from time to time ordain and establish." On the basis of these provisions the Supreme Court in *Ex parte McCardle*[58] and in *Sheldon v. Sill*[59] seemed to suggest that Congress was free to limit both the Court's own appellate authority and the jurisdiction of the lower courts however it pleased.

The holdings of these decisions, however, were far less sweeping. *Sheldon* upheld the Assignee Clause of the 1789 Judiciary Act, a minor adjustment to the diversity jurisdiction designed to prevent persons with local controversies from manufacturing federal jurisdiction by

---

[58]74 U.S. 506 (1869).
[59]49 U.S. 441 (1850).

assigning causes of action to citizens of other states. *McCardle* upheld the power of Congress to repeal an 1867 provision that gave the Supreme Court jurisdiction to review judgments in certain habeas corpus cases. But the Court was careful to point out that the repeal did not affect other provisions authorizing review of the same decisions. Indeed, in *Ex parte Yerger*,[60] later the same term, the Court upheld its jurisdiction to review a denial of habeas corpus on petition for habeas corpus and certiorari under the All Writs Act.

In *Lauf v. Shinner*[61] the Supreme Court upheld the Norris-LaGuardia Act, which deprived federal courts of jurisdiction to issue injunctions in certain labor disputes, saying only that "there can be no question of the power of Congress thus to define and limit the jurisdiction" of the federal courts. But this decision need not stand for plenary authority over federal jurisdiction either, because today at least there is no doubt that on the merits it was perfectly proper to abolish the labor injunction.

*Lockerty v. Phillips*[62] upheld Congress's power to give the Emergency Court of Appeals exclusive jurisdiction over suits attacking the validity of regulations under a wartime price-control statute. This was simply a venue mea-

---

[60]49 U.S. 441 (1850).
[61]303 U.S. 323 (1938).
[62]319 U.S. 182 (1943).

sure: Other federal courts were closed, the state courts were closed, but one federal court was open, and the Supreme Court could review its decisions. *Yakus v. United States*[63] is more troublesome, for it upheld a provision forbidding a criminal defendant to argue in defense to a prosecution for violating price regulations that the regulations themselves were invalid. Yet the reason for this conclusion was that Congress had provided what the Court considered a fair opportunity to raise the defense in advance of the criminal prosecution by suing in the Emergency Court of Appeals. The decision was thus based on the familiar notion that a litigant who fails to take advantage of existing remedies may forfeit the opportunity to make a later case. The precedents, therefore, do not establish any broad congressional power to take away federal jurisdiction.

Several arguments have been made against the existence of such an unlimited power. One approach is typified by a dictum in *Martin v. Hunter's Lessee*[64] attempting to reconcile the various clauses of Article III. It was true, Justice Story acknowledged, that neither the lower courts nor the Supreme Court need be given jurisdiction over all cases or controversies falling within that Article. Yet the first clause of the Article was mandatory: The entire federal judicial power

---

[63]321 U.S. 414 (1944).
[64]14 U.S. 304 (1816).

must be vested in some federal court. Thus
Congress might make exceptions to the Supreme
Court's appellate jurisdiction only if it gave
jurisdiction over the excepted cases to the
inferior federal courts, and vice-versa.

This argument was accepted by the District of
Columbia Circuit in *Eisentrager v. Forrestal*,[65]
but it has never reflected the actual state of the
law. No federal tribunal, for example, has ever
had jurisdiction over diversity cases involving
less that the jurisdictional amount, and it is
difficult to see why the framers would have
wanted to forbid such an obviously appropriate
means of conserving judicial resources.

One passage in the *Martin* opinion would
limit the mandatory nature of Article III to those
categories (i.e., federal-question and admiralty
cases and those involving foreign diplomats) in
which the judicial power is expressly extended to
"all" cases, but that makes little sense either: It
would permit Congress effectively to neutralize
judicial review by giving exclusive authority
over constitutional cases to a single court se-
lected for its sympathy with congressional aims.

A second argument in the *Eisentrager*
opinion was more promising. Article I, § 9
forbids Congress to suspend the writ of habeas
corpus except under certain stringent

---

[65] 174 F.2d 961 (1949).

conditions; Congress would offend this provision if it closed all courts to certain habeas corpus claims.

The Second Circuit generalized this principle in upholding the so-called Portal-to-Portal Act in *Battaglia v. General Motors Corp.* in 1948.[66] The Supreme Court in an earlier decision had given a surprisingly broad reading to the Fair Labor Standards Act, creating a windfall benefit for employees and an enormous unexpected burden on employers. Congress then amended the statute to abolish this liability retroactively. In an effort to avoid judicial review of the repeal, Congress further provided that no court, federal or state, should have jurisdiction to enforce the preexisting law.

The Second Circuit had no difficulty in upholding the repeal on the merits despite a claim that it destroyed vested rights in violation of the Due Process Clause. However, the court was not deterred from reaching the merits by the additional provision taking away jurisdiction. For in the court's view the power of Congress to limit jurisdiction, like all its other powers, was subject to the restrictions of due process.

This argument seems equally applicable to other limitations on congressional power: To close all courts to a valid constitutional claim ef-

---

[66]169 F.2d 254.

fectively denies the substantive constitutional right. This argument derives strength from the judicial-guardian theory of *Marbury v. Madison*: Judicial review is an essential tool for keeping other branches of government from exceeding their constitutional authority.

Whether this argument requires that federal as contrasted with state courts be open, or whether the Supreme Court itself must have jurisdiction over constitutional cases, is not so plain. That federal courts would maintain the uniformity and supremacy of federal law, however, was clearly the expectation of the Constitutional Convention, and the focus of that expectation was the Supreme Court. On this view Congress's power to make exceptions to the Supreme Court's appellate jurisdiction permits only minor procedural adjustments like the Assignee Clause and the jurisdictional amount; in the words of Professor Henry Hart, it was not designed to destroy "the essential role of the Supreme Court in the constitutional plan."

One final Supreme Court decision deserves mention, for it is often cited as having struck down a statute that limited federal jurisdiction. A Reconstruction statute permitted recovery of property seized by the United States during the Civil War upon proof that the owner had not given aid or comfort to the rebellion, and the Supreme Court had held that such proof could be made by producing a Presidential pardon. Congress then amended the statute to provide that a pardon was instead to be taken as proof that the owner had given aid and comfort to the rebellion, and it deprived all courts of jurisdiction to return property to a person with a pardon. In *United States v. Klein*[67] the Court held the amended statute unconstitutional, arguing that Congress had attempted to dictate the result in pending cases and to use its power over jurisdiction to deny substantive rights.

Both of these points could equally have been made in *McCardle*, where the restriction of jurisdiction was upheld. One important difference, not noted by the opinion, was that in *Klein*, in contrast to *McCardle*, all avenues of recovery were closed. To respect the jurisdictional repeal therefore arguably would effectively have denied the substantive right to the full effect of a pardon. Thus *Klein*, like the Second Circuit's opinion in *Battaglia*, arguably stands as authority that the power to control jurisdiction may not be so exercised as to close all courts to a valid constitutional claim.

A narrower interpretation of *Klein*, however, was suggested by Justice Rutledge's dissenting opinion in *Yakus v United States*, which is mentioned above. It was one thing, said Rutledge, simply to take away jurisdiction; it was quite another to give a court jurisdiction and direct it to ignore the Constitution in making its

---

[67]80 U.S. 128 (1872).

decision. For to do that would offend even the narrow clean-hands aspect of *Marbury*: At a minimum the judges themselves must follow the Constitution. It is possible to interpret *Klein* as an application of this principle. For the statute in that case required the Supreme Court upon proof of a pardon to dismiss not the appeal but the cause itself – that is, to exercise jurisdiction and reverse the judgment of the court below.

## 2. Legislative Courts

Quite distinct from the issue just discussed is the question whether power that Article III says shall be vested in the federal courts may be given to other federal agencies.

Article III not only provides that federal judicial authority be vested in courts; it specifies that the judges of those courts "shall hold their offices during good behavior" and that their salaries "shall not be diminished during their continuance in office." The purpose of these provisions, as the Court has repeatedly acknowledged and as Hamilton made clear in the Federalist, is to ensure the independence of the judges.

The notion of "legislative" courts free from Article III restrictions got its start in *American*

*Ins. Co. v. Canter*,[68] a maritime action for salvage in a court created by the legislature of the Territory of Florida. It was argued that, because the case fell within the judicial power as defined by the Constitution, jurisdiction could not be given to any federal tribunal that did not satisfy the requirements of Article III. The Supreme Court rejected the argument, holding that the Florida court had been created not under Article III but pursuant to the provision of Article IV authorizing Congress to make rules for the government of the territories.

Later cases extended this principle to military courts, to consular courts in foreign countries, and, more recently, to local courts in the District of Columbia.[69] All these instances involved extraordinary situations in which it could plausibly be argued that it was unlikely the framers had intended to burden the system with judges enjoying tenure during good behavior.

*Ex parte Bakelite Corp.*,[70] however, went much further in holding that the Court of Customs Appeals could exercise nonjudicial authority because it had been created pursuant to Congress's power to lay and collect taxes and not under Article III. Since Congress could have provided for the collection of customs duties without employing any judicial process at all,

---

[68] 26 U.S. 516 (1828).
[69] Palmore v. United States, 410 U.S. 963 (1973).
[70] 279 U.S. 438 (1929).

the Court reasoned, it could take the lesser step of creating a court for this purpose that was not protected by the safeguards of Article III.

The premise of this argument seems questionable enough; even where due process permits seizure of property without prior hearing, it generally requires an opportunity for subsequent redress. But the conclusion ignores the plain language of the Constitution. Article III may not require the creation of inferior federal courts, but it flatly demands that, if there is to be a federal court, its judges have tenure during good behavior.

Nevertheless the *Bakelite* decision did not break down the tenure requirement entirely. The Court was careful to point out that "legislative" courts could be given jurisdiction only over cases involving "public rights," that is to say only when Congress could provide for resolution of the controversy entirely outside the courts, and only when the Government was a party. "Inherently judicial" controversies, whatever they might be, could be entrusted within the federal system only to regular federal courts.

*Crowell v. Benson*,[71] however, undermined the Article III requirements still further. Congress having established an administrative tribunal to pass upon maritime workers' com-

---

[71]285 U.S. 22 (1932).

pensation claims, it was argued that Article III required de novo review of factual determinations made by that tribunal. The Court agreed only with respect to certain facts which it deemed to be both jurisdictional and constitutional, namely whether the injured party was an "employee" and whether the injury occurred on navigable waters. With respect to other determinations, the Court added in dictum, no such intensive reexamination was required. Thus after *Crowell*, even in a case admitted to be inherently judicial – a private controversy over compensation for personal injury – most factual decisions could be committed to an administrative commission subject only to limited judicial review. In other words, after *Crowell v. Benson* the constitutional requirements of life tenure and irreducible salary for judges "both of the supreme and inferior courts" appeared to apply only to those of the appellate courts.

The Supreme Court breathed new life into the tenure and salary provisions in *Northern Pipeline Construction Co. v. Marathon Pipeline Co.* in 1982,[72] striking down a statute that had entrusted the entire bankruptcy jurisdiction of the district courts to bankruptcy judges appointed for fourteen years. The only exceptions from Article III's requirements, wrote Justice Brennan for four Justices, were for territorial and military tribunals and for public rights.

---

[72]458 U.S. 50.

While some aspects of bankruptcy (such as the right to a discharge of debts) might fall into this last category, a common-law contract action by the bankrupt did not. In other cases, Brennan continued, nontenured officers could function only as "adjuncts" subject to de novo judicial review, as in the case of federal magistrates.[73]

The difficulty with this line of reasoning was to distinguish *Crowell v. Benson*, which had seemed to permit more limited judicial oversight in a case of private right. Justice Brennan's effort to distinguish *Crowell* on the ground that the statute in that case provided for more intensive judicial review seemed inconsistent with *Crowell* itself; his alternative argument that Congress was free to entrust decision of federal statutory claims to nontenured judges because it need not pass the statute at all contradicted clear precedents respecting both due process and the civil jury and seemed to ignore the doctrine of unconstitutional conditions. For as every law student knows, the greater power does not always include the lesser.

Two Justices concurred in the result without giving reasons, and later decisions showed that *Northern Pipeline* had not been a major victory after all. *Thomas v. Union Carbide Agricultural Products Co.*[74] upheld a provision

---

[73]See United States v. Raddatz, 447 U.S. 667 (1980).
[74]473 U.S. 568 (1985).

for compulsory arbitration of private disputes over allocation of the costs of pesticide registration, arguing that the right to compensation in such a case bore "many of the characteristics of a public right'" because it served a public purpose. *Commodity Futures Trading Commission v. Schor*[75] upheld the authority of an administrative commission to entertain a state-law counterclaim against a party who had filed a complaint seeking reparations from his broker: Whatever Justice Brennan had said in *Northern Pipeline*, it mattered neither that the right was private nor that it had been created by state law, and the plaintiff had effectively consented to the counterclaim by filing his own complaint with the commission.

Given *Northern Pipeline*, it seems fair to say that something still remains of the constitutional provision for independent judges; but it is not easy to say how much.

### 3. Article I Powers in Article III Courts

The issue in *National Mutual Ins. Co. v. Tidewater Transfer Co.*[76] was the validity of a 1940 statute purporting to give the federal courts jurisdiction of controversies between citizens of

---

[75]478 U.S. 833 (1986).
[76]337 U.S. 582 (1949).

the District of Columbia and citizens of a state. Seven of the Justices said this could not be done under Article III. Six of them said it could not be done under any other article. Nevertheless the statute was upheld by a vote of five to four.

Justices Rutledge and Murphy were straight-forward about it: Article III allowed jurisdiction of controversies between citizens of different states, and the word "state" was broad enough to include the District of Columbia. There was the same need for jurisdiction in a diversity case involving District of Columbia citizens as there was in any other diversity case, namely to pro-tect out-of-state litigants from the danger of local bias. The remaining Justices said "states" meant "states," those political entities that had the right to elect Senators and Representatives under Article I. Chief Justice Marshall had con-firmed this conclusion in an 1804 case holding that a District of Columbia citizen was not a cit-izen of a state within the meaning of the 1789 statutory provision.

Justice Jackson, for the other three Justices in the majority, attempted to justify the jurisdiction of an Article III court on the basis of Article I. That Article, as he pointed out, gave Congress the power of "exclusive legislation" over the District of Columbia. That authority, he concluded, empowered Congress to establish courts for Dis-trict citizens; and it was immaterial whether it gave jurisdiction in such cases to an Article I or an Article III court. Six Justices disagreed: The

Court had held any number of times that Congress could give no powers to an Article III court beyond those enumerated in Article III.

As Jackson argued, the precedents to this effect fell into two categories: The courts could resolve neither nonjudicial matters nor controversies exclusively of state concern. The first category reflected separation-of-powers concerns, the second those of federalism. Neither was a problem in *Tidewater*. For the controversy before the court was a garden-variety judicial controversy between adverse parties, and it can hardly be argued that providing courts for District of Columbia citizens is a peculiarly state function in light of the general grant of congressional power over the District of Columbia.

Nevertheless, a majority of the Court concluded that Congress could not give Article I powers to Article III courts, and rightly so. For it is only the "judicial power of the United States" that Article III permits to be vested in these courts, and the case was not within that power. This conclusion may appear peculiar in light of the concession that Congress could create an Article I tribunal to hear this kind of case; but that is a criticism to be directed at the framers of the Constitution.

# II. FEDERAL-QUESTION CASES

Article III extends the judicial power to "Cases . . . arising under this Constitution, the laws of the United States, and treaties." Since 1875 the statute (now 28 U.S.C. § 1331) has given the district courts jurisdiction, of "civil actions" that "arise under the Constitution, laws, or treaties of the United States." Important questions of interpretation have arisen under both the constitutional and the statutory provisions.

## A. IDENTIFYING FEDERAL-QUESTION CASES

### 1. Constitutional Scope

The landmark case on the constitutional definition of cases "arising under" federal law is *Osborn v. Bank of the United States* (1824).[1] The statute that created the Bank made it "able and capable . . . to sue and be sued . . . in any Circuit Court of the United States." Though this statute appeared only to give the Bank legal capacity, the Court held it gave the circuit courts jurisdiction of all suits by or against the Bank and that as so construed it was constitutional; for all such suits arose under federal law.

By modern standards, at least, *Osborn* itself was an easy case for federal jurisdiction. The Bank sued to enjoin the collection of a state tax

---

[1] 22 U.S. 738.

on the ground of intergovernmental immunity; its complaint was based entirely on federal law. A companion case, however, turned on a contract dispute that the Court did not suggest was federal; the Court said it was enough that federal law determined the bank's existence and its capacity to contract.

In dissent, Justice William Johnson criticized the Court for holding that federal jurisdiction existed in every case in which there was a *potential* federal question. That indeed would have been an untenable interpretation, since there is a potential federal question in nearly every case: One can always argue that the state law under which the suit is brought is invalid. But the opinion did not rest on the possibility that a federal question might be raised; its premise was that every claim by or against the Bank was based in part on federal law. In the contract case, for example, the Bank's capacity to contract was an indispensable ingredient of the plaintiff's claim.

Johnson's response that a challenge to the Bank's long-established federal authority would be frivolous and thus unlikely confuses the existence of a federal *question* with that of a federal *claim*. Federal jurisdiction is based not only on the need for uniform interpretation of federal law but also on the necessity to enforce federal rights; Johnson conceded that the Bank might have difficulty vindicating those rights in a hostile state court.

The Court extended *Osborn* to ordinary tort actions against federally incorporated railroads in the *Pacific Railroad Removal Cases*[2] in 1885. Its next significant encounter with the *Osborn* problem came in *Textile Workers Union v. Lincoln Mills* in 1957.[3]

Section 301 of the Taft-Hartley Act gives the district courts jurisdiction of actions involving labor contracts affecting interstate commerce. Concluding that this provision implicitly gave the courts power to create federal substantive law governing such contracts, the Court had no difficulty in upholding its constitutionality. Given the Court's interpretation, § 301 actions arose under federal law in the most traditional sense; the entire cause of action was federal.

Unable to discover any such authorization to create federal common law, Justice Frankfurter concluded in dissent that the statute was unconstitutional: Congress had attempted to give the federal courts jurisdiction over cases arising under state law. Conceding that the union's authority to represent an entire bargaining unit might constitute a federal "ingredient" in a § 301 action, he thought that insufficient: The *Railroad Removal Cases* had been, he said, a "sport" (i.e., wrongly decided), and *Osborn* should be understood as a suit by the United

---

[2]115 U.S. 1.
[3]353 U.S. 448.

States, since the Bank was a federal instrumentality.

Occasional commentators, agreeing that § 301 did not create substantive federal law, attempted to uphold it on a theory of "protective" jurisdiction. Congress had undisputed power under the Commerce Clause to provide substantive law governing contracts affecting interstate commerce. That being so, the argument ran, Congress could take the lesser step – less intrusive on state interests, that is – of granting federal jurisdiction without creating federal substantive law.

As Justice Frankfurter noted, however, the greater power does not necessarily include the lesser; there is such a thing as the doctrine of unconstitutional conditions. He never said why the greater did not include the lesser in *Lincoln Mills*, but we can help him. Absent federal law there is no need for uniformity and no federal right to vindicate; the case does not come within the purposes of federal-question jurisdiction. Nor does it fall within the terms of Article III. To say that a case arises under federal law whenever a federal statute gives jurisdiction would destroy all limitations on federal court authority.

## 2. Remote Federal Issues

*T.B. Harms Co. v. Eliscu*[4] was an action to determine the ownership of a copyright. The copyright itself had been created by federal law; the plaintiff could not prevail without establishing its validity. Thus, as in *Osborn*, there was a federal ingredient in the plaintiff's claim; Congress could give jurisdiction over such a case if it chose. Nevertheless the Second Circuit held there was no jurisdiction; the case did not arise under the copyright laws within the meaning of the statute (28 U.S.C. § 1338). Thus a case may arise under federal law for constitutional purposes and not under the statute; the court interpreted the words of the statute more narrowly than the identical words of Article III.

This conclusion was in accord with long-standing Supreme Court precedent. In the Western states, for example, most land titles are derived from the United States. In a dispute over current ownership of the land, a deed from the Federal Government is thus an ingredient of every claim, and again *Osborn* would support a grant of federal jurisdiction. When both parties claim under the same original grant, however, the chances that either will challenge it are pretty slim, and the same was true of the copyright in *Harms*. The real dispute in such cases typically concerns some later transaction governed by state law; the federal ingredient is too remote to support jurisdiction under the statute.

---

[4]339 F.2d 823 (2d Cir. 1964).

As Professor Mishkin has explained, it is essential that Congress have power to give jurisdiction over all cases in which there is a federal ingredient. State hostility to the Bank, for example, was such that even Supreme Court review of state court decisions might not have sufficed to protect it against effective evisceration of its power to contract. On the other hand, it is not likely that Congress, in using the same words in the statute, meant to draw into the federal courts a vast quantity of litigation almost certain to turn on issues of state law.

For similar reasons the statute itself (28 U.S.C. § 1349) provides that the mere fact that a corporation was established under federal law is not a sufficient basis for arising-under jurisdiction unless the United States owns over half the capital stock.

### 3. The Well-Pleaded Complaint Rule

A further important limitation on statutory federal-question jurisdiction is illustrated by *Louisville & Nashville R.R. v. Mottley*.[5] Ms. Mottley sued for breach of a contract to provide free passes, alleging that the railroad's refusal to perform was based upon a federal statute outlawing such passes but that that statute was unconstitutional. Although two federal questions

---

[5]211 U.S. 149 (1908).

had thus been presented and decided below, the Supreme Court held there was no jurisdiction because Ms. Mottley was anticipating a federal defense and reply: The "plaintiff's statement of his own cause of action" must be based upon federal law.

The administration of this "well-pleaded complaint" rule has been based upon a highly technical reading of the rules of pleading. When owners of a federal mining patent sued to *remove a cloud* on their title, jurisdiction was upheld because the invalidity of the competing federal claim was an "essential part of the plaintiffs' cause of action";[6] yet a bill to *quiet* title in a similar situation was dismissed because the plaintiff in such an action was not required to allege the nature of the adverse claim.[7]

In *Skelly Oil Co. v. Phillips Petroleum Co.*[8] a contract to purchase gas was conditioned on the issuance of a certificate of public convenience and necessity by the Federal Power Commission, and the buyer sued for a declaratory judgment that the condition had been met. Although it appears that the plaintiff had the burden of alleging that the certificate was satisfactory, the Court held the action did not arise under federal law. The Declaratory Judgment Act was not

---

[6]Hopkins v. Walker, 244 U.S. 486 (1917).
[7]Marshall v. Desert Properties Co., 103 F.2d 551 (9th Cir. 1939).
[8]339 U.S. 667 (1950).

intended to extend the jurisdiction of the District Courts, but only to provide an additional remedy in cases already within their authority. Thus the Court applied the *Mottley* test not to the declaratory complaint that had actually been filed but to a complaint that *might* have been filed in a hypothetical action for damages or injunction based on the same facts. In such a case breach of the condition would have been a defense and its anticipation would not have supported federal-question jurisdiction; and thus the court had no authority to entertain the request for declaratory relief, as the American Law Institute not so long ago proposed.

The roundabout test of the *Skelly* case greatly complicates the jurisdictional inquiry. Moreover, a central purpose of the *Mottley* rule was to permit jurisdiction to be settled at the out-set, not left in limbo while waiting to see whether or not an anticipated defense is raised. This pur-pose would be satisfied by looking to the actual declaratory complaint.

But the *Mottley* rule has another and more far-reaching consequence. Not only does it exclude federal jurisdiction based upon the prediction that a federal defense or reply may later be presented; because § 1441(a) limits removal from state courts to cases "of which the district courts . . . have original jurisdiction," neither party may remove even when such a defense or reply is actually made. As Professor Wechsler once argued, the statute appears to have got it backwards: A defendant is permitted to remove when the plaintiff needs a federal forum, but not when he needs one himself.

The ALI proposal would have allowed removal on the basis of certain federal issues actually raised after the complaint, but subject to significant restrictions. The federal issue must be "dispositive" of the action; collateral matters like the amount of damages or the admissibility of evidence would not do. Neither would constitutional objections to service of process, choice of law, or the failure to respect a prior judgment; and removal could be based only on federal claims made in an answer, not in a reply.

If the ALI agreed with Professor Wechsler that defendants as well as plaintiffs had an interest in federal determination of their federal rights, why did it make such a parsimonious proposal? The ALI's reservations reflect the fact that the relative dominance of state law is likely to increase as the federal claim is raised later in the proceeding or is more remote from the merits of the case. Thus *Mottley* may be based as much on federalism concerns as on the need to resolve jurisdiction early. And thus there may be something to say for *Skelly* after all, for state issues do not disappear simply because the parties are reversed.

Ordinarily the contention that federal law preempts a state claim is a defense, and under *Mottley* the case does not arise under federal law. But in *Avco Corp. v. Aero Lodge*[9] the Court upheld federal jurisdiction over a complaint seeking to enforce a no-strike clause in a collective-bargaining contract. Even though the plaintiff had not invoked federal law, wrote Justice Douglas, under *Lincoln Mills* the governing law was federal; and thus the case arose under federal law. The Court's later attempt to explain this decision in terms of "complete" preemption[10] was an invitation to confusion; the basis of decision was that the plaintiff's cause of action was federal. Even on this basis the *Avco* decision seems questionable; *Mottley* and § 1441 tell us there is no need for a federal trial forum to protect the defendant's interests, and if the plaintiff chooses not to assert a federal claim I see no reason to force it upon him.

In *Verlinden B.V. v. Central Bank of Nigeria*[11] the Supreme Court held that Congress could constitutionally give the district courts jurisdiction of an action by an alien against a foreign state: Since sovereign immunity and its exceptions depended on federal statute, "every action against a foreign sovereign necessarily involves application of a body of substantive federal law." It was immaterial that immunity was a defense and its exceptions a matter to be raised by reply: The well-pleaded-complaint rule was

---

[9]390 U.S. 557 (1968).
[10]Franchise Tax Board v. Construction Laborers Vacation Trust, 463 U.S. 1 (1983).
[11]461 U.S. 480 (1983).

an interpretation of the jurisdictional statute,
and in this respect too Congress's power was
broader.

### 4. Incorporation of Federal or State Law

In *Smith v. Kansas City Title & Trust Co.*[12] a
shareholder sued to enjoin his company from in-
vesting in bonds issued by a federal agency on
the ground that the statute authorizing issuance
of the bonds was unconstitutional. The Supreme
Court upheld jurisdiction because "the right to
relief depend[ed] upon the construction or application of the Constitution . . . of the United
States." Justice Holmes, dissenting, protested
that the cause of action arose under Missouri
law, which created both the obligation to invest
only in lawful securities and the right of a
shareholder to sue to enforce it: "The mere adoption by a state law of a United States law as a
criterion or test, when the law of the United States
has no force *proprio vigore*, does not cause a case
under the state law to be also a case under the law
of the United States."

*Moore v. Chesapeake & Ohio Ry.*[13] was an action for damages for personal injury suffered as
a result of violation of the Federal Safety Appli-
ance Act, which imposes a duty to employ certain

---

[12]255 U.S. 180 (1921).
[13]291 U.S. 205 (1934).

safety devices on trains employed by interstate carriers but which at the time created no right of action for damages. The plaintiff sued on the theory that a Kentucky statute provided a remedy for injuries caused by violations of the federal statute. The Supreme Court held the action did not arise under federal law for purposes of an action in the district court, while conceding that questions as to the scope of the federal act were federal questions reviewable by the Supreme Court when identical damage actions were brought in state court.

It is not easy to reconcile these decisions. In *Moore* as well as *Smith* the result turned upon construction of federal law; in neither case did federal law provide a remedy.

The *Smith* test for determining whether a case arises under federal law seems obviously overbroad. If a state adopted the Federal Rules of Civil Procedure for its own courts and followed federal decisions in construing them, every interpretation of the state rules would depend upon federal law. But Congress has never attempted to prescribe how state courts conduct their proceedings; state adoption of federal standards creates neither a federal right to enforce nor a federal interest in how the matter is resolved. Nor should it matter, as the Court suggested in *Moore,* whether the question is district-court jurisdiction or Supreme Court review.

*Moore* and *Smith* differ from the preceding example in that federal law allegedly applied of its own force in those cases to invalidate the bonds and to impose duties on the railroad. One commentator would make this difference decisive: A case arises under federal law if that law creates the duty sued upon, even if state law provides the remedy. Even in such a case, however, the failure of Congress to provide a remedy means there is no federal right to recover and suggests federal indifference to the outcome of the suit.

The Supreme Court returned to this vexing problem in 1986 in *Merrell Dow Pharmaceuticals, Inc. v. Thompson,*[14] where the plaintiffs sought damages under state law for alleged misbranding of medication under the Federal Food, Drug, and Cosmetic Act. Justice Brennan argued in dissent that there was a federal interest in hearing the case to assure uniformity of the governing federal standard, but the majority was not impressed. When Congress chooses not to provide a federal cause of action, wrote Justice Stevens, it impliedly precludes federal jurisdiction over state claims based upon the federal duty.

My own view is that the absence of a federal remedy indicates indifference rather than hostility to the availability of private suit; but

---

[14]291 U.S. 205 (1934).

indifference should be enough to negate any federal interest in the outcome of the case. In any event, since the decision was explicitly based upon the perceived desires of Congress in enacting the substantive statute, *Merrell Dow* seems not to provide a definitive answer to all questions of state incorporation of federal law. It appears to say nothing, for example, about a case like *Smith*, in which a state provides a remedy for alleged violation of the Constitution.

The converse situation has also presented jurisdictional problems. Many federal statutes, while creating rights of action, refer to state law to define the federal right. Thus the Copyright Act, for example, gives a right of renewal to the "widow" of a deceased author, and the Court has held that widowhood is to be determined by state law.

In a comparable case involving federal land the Supreme Court once held there was no jurisdiction. A federal statute authorized the issuance of patents for mining claims on federal land and provided for proceedings to resolve conflicting claims, which were to be determined to a large extent by "local customs or rules of miners." "The recognition by Congress of local customs and statutory provisions as at times controlling the right of possession" said the Court in *Shoshone Mining Co. v. Rutter*,[15] "does not

---

[15]177 U.S. 505 (1900).

incorporate them into the body of Federal law."
This conclusion seems erroneous. Since both the
right and the remedy were created by federal
law, the fact that certain matters were to be
decided as state law would decide them does not
seem to indicate a lack of federal interest in the
case, any more than a state would be without
concern as to the operation of its own courts
merely because it had incorporated the federal
rules.

Attempts to enunciate a general test for determining which cases arise under federal law
have universally failed. *Smith*'s suggestion that
there is jurisdiction whenever federal law must
be construed is not only too broad; it would also
exclude cases in which federal law is clear, although a basic purpose of federal jurisdiction is
to provide a forum for the enforcement of federal
rights. Holmes's test of the law that created the
cause of action is of no help in those cases in
which it is most needed, namely, when part of the
cause is created by federal and part by state law.
It is insufficient under *Merrell Dow* that the duty
is federal and under *Shoshone* that the remedy
is; to hold the remedy decisive would make every
case filed under the Declaratory Judgment Act a
federal-question case, although otherwise based
entirely on state law. In proposing a
comprehensive revision of the statutes, the ALI
made no effort to define cases arising under
federal law; Professor William Cohen has advocated a "pragmatic" test based largely upon the
relative dominance of state and federal issues

and the need for sympathy or expertise in the application of federal law.

It may be more helpful to bear in mind the categories of cases in which federal jurisdiction has been denied despite the arguable presence of a federal question. First there is the statutory requirement that the federal matter form part of the plaintiff's own claim. Second, as a matter of statutory construction, such remote federal issues as the validity of an original land grant or copyright will not suffice in a controversy over later transactions in the same property, even if the plaintiff must allege them. Finally, the courts will sometimes refuse jurisdiction when state law incorporates federal for state purposes, or, perhaps less justifiably, when a federal statute incorporates state law.

## B. SUPPLEMENTAL JURISDICTION

It is the presence of a federal claim that gives rise to federal-question jurisdiction. But the statute grants jurisdiction over "civil actions," not claims, and the Constitution extends the judicial power to "cases" arising under federal law. Thus from the beginning there have been situations in which federal courts have had jurisdiction not only over federal questions but also over related state-law issues that constitute part of the same "case" or "civil action."

The Court upheld this authority early as 1824, in *Osborn v. Bank of the United States*.[16] In the companion contract case, as the Court noted, federal and state elements combined to create a single claim; if the Court had not assumed power to adjudicate state-law questions, it could not have acted at all.

The modern doctrine of supplemental jurisdiction, which derives from the 1966 decision in *United Mine Workers v. Gibbs*,[17] is broader. *Gibbs* arose out of a labor dispute; the plaintiff alleged that the defendant's acts offended both federal and state law. In contrast to the contract case considered in *Osborn*, the federal claim could have been decided alone; yet the Court held the district court could decide the state claim too in order to avoid a separate state proceeding: Because "the state and federal claims . . . derive[d] from a common nucleus of operative fact," they were part of the same constitutional "case."

Following this lead, most courts of appeals held that the doctrine permitted claims against parties not named in the original complaint, so long as the *Gibbs* test was met. The policy of judicial economy that underlay the doctrine appeared to justify this conclusion, and there were analogies in "ancillary" jurisdiction over

---

[16]22 U.S. 738.
[17]22 U.S. 738.

nondiverse parties impleaded or interpleaded in actions between citizens of different states. But *Zahn v. International Paper Co.*,[18] by refusing to allow "pendent" jurisdiction over additional class members whose claims did not meet the jurisdictional amount, seemed to suggest that allegedly pendent state-law claims made against additional parties were not part of the same "civil action" and thus could not be entertained.

The Supreme Court confirmed this suggestion by a 5-4 vote in *Finley v. United States*,[19] holding that the plaintiff in an action against the United States under the Federal Tort Claims Act could not join a state-law claim against a private party for the same injury. Congress promptly responded by amending the statutes to reverse the Court's decision. With exceptions noted in chapter 4, § 1367(a) now provides that, in any action of which they have original jurisdiction,

> the district courts shall have supplemental jurisdiction over all other claims that are so related to claims in the action within such original jurisdiction that they form part of the same case or controversy under Article III of the United States Constitution. Such supplemental jurisdiction shall include claims that involve the joinder or intervention of additional parties.

---

[18]22 U.S. 738.
[19]490 U.S. 545(1989).

As *Gibbs* had said, the doctrine is discretionary; the court may refuse to entertain supplemental claims if state law is complex, if state-law claims predominate, or if the federal claims are dismissed before trial.

In cases in which federal law authorizes nationwide service of process there is another dimension to the problem: whether supplemental jurisdiction can cure defects of service of process or venue. The lower courts are in conflict on this issue, and the Supreme Court has not spoken. When the supplemental claim is against the original defendant, there is a strong argument that judicial economy should prevail. Since the defendant must already appear to litigate the federal claim, the burden of litigating related state-law matters in the same forum should not be substantial; and the principles applied in *Van Dusen v. Barrack* (infra p. xxx), should prevent any adverse choice-of-law consequences from the change of forum. Whether the court should be able to dispense with ordinary service and venue requirements in order to include additional parties, however, seems doubtful.

When state and federal claims joined in state court are sufficiently related that the entire action could have been filed in federal court under § 1371(a), the defendant may remove the whole case under the general removal provision, 28 U.S.C. § 1441(a). If an unrelated state claim is joined with the federal claim in state court, the latter should be removable either as a separate "civil action" under that provision or under § 1441(c), which permits removal when "a separate and independent claim" is joined with other claims in a state court.

# III. ADMIRALTY

Federal district courts have had jurisdiction over admiralty and maritime cases ever since 1789; the present statute is 28 U.S.C. § 1333.

In England the admiralty jurisdiction was restricted to tidewaters, and the Supreme Court initially construed the statute in accord with this practice.[1] As inland commerce expanded, however, Congress passed an act extending admiralty to the Great Lakes and their connecting waters, and the Court upheld it in *The Genesee Chief*[2] in 1851. Congress could not enlarge the constitutional scope of the jurisdiction, the Court said, but its interpretation was persuasive: For all relevant purposes the lakes were just like the ocean. Subsequent decisions extended the jurisdiction to other lakes, rivers, and even canals, so long as they constituted part of a continuous water route to other states or nations.

The test of admiralty jurisdiction in contract cases, sensibly enough, has been whether or not the contract is related to maritime commerce. The place the contract was made or to be performed is immaterial. Oddly enough, contracts to build or to sell ships have traditionally been excluded from the jurisdiction, as were ship mortgages until Congress enacted the Ship

---

[1]The Thomas Jefferson, 23 U.S. 428 (1825).
[2]53 U.S. 443.

Mortgage Act, which the Supreme Court upheld in *The Thomas Barlum*[3] in 1934.

In tort cases the traditional rule was that jurisdiction existed only if the tort occurred on navigable waters. Moreover, as in conventional choice-of-law cases, the tort was said to occur not where the wrongful act was committed but where the injury was suffered.[4] Thus when a ship collided with a drawbridge the shipowner could sue in admiralty but the bridge owner could not, since the bridge was considered an extension of the land.

To remedy this situation Congress enacted the Admiralty Extension Act (46 U.S.C. § 740) in 1948. The Act extends the jurisdiction to injuries caused by a vessel on land, and lower courts have upheld it, citing *The Genesee Chief*. The Supreme Court, without discussing the validity of the statute, has sensibly held it applicable to harm done by a ship's crew or its cargo as well as by the ship itself.[5] Most recently, in *Jerome H. Grubart, Inc. v. Great Lakes Dredge & Dock Co.*,[6] the Court applied the Extension Act to uphold admiralty jurisdiction over claims for damage caused when construction equipment on a barge repairing navigational structures in the Chicago

---

[3]293 U.S. 21.
[4]The Plymouth, 70 U.S. 20 (1866).
[5]Gutierrez v. Waterman S.S. Corp., 373 U.S. 206 (1963).
[6]513 U.S. 527 (1995).

River punctured a tunnel and caused flooding in basements in downtown Chicago.

The Extension Act applies only to injuries caused by vessels, and in cases not involving ships the shoreline continues to produce arbitrary distinctions. The Sixth Circuit held a suit on behalf of a man who had *fallen* into the water was not maritime because the wrong had occurred when he tripped on the pier;[7] yet when the victim had *dived* from the pier the same court held the tort had not occurred until he landed in navigable waters.[8]

The Extension Act was held not to enlarge the scope of federal workers' compensation under the Longshore and Harbor Workers' Compensation Act, which covered only injuries suffered "upon . . . navigable waters."[9] Congress responded by extending compensation to injuries suffered by "maritime" employees on adjoining piers or other areas "customarily used" in servicing vessels, whether or not they were caused by the ship.

The Supreme Court has extended two seamen's remedies for personal injury shoreward without benefit of statute by classifying them es-

---

[7]Wiper v. Great Lakes Engineering Works, 340 F.2d 727 (1965).

[8]Chapman v. City of Grosse Pointe Farms, 385 F.2d 962 (1967).

[9]Nacirema Operating Co. v. Johnson, 396 U.S. 212 (1969).

sentially as contractual: Jones Act damages for negligence[10] and maintenance and cure.[11] The Court's refusal to allow tort recovery by a long-shoreman injured by his own truck on the pier,[12] however, appears to have put an end to such innovations.

Just as in some of the cases discussed above the locality test was too narrow to satisfy the purposes of admiralty jurisdiction, in others it was too broad. Finally resolving a conflict of authority in 1972, the Supreme Court in *Executive Jet Aviation, Inc. v. City of Cleveland*[13] refused jurisdiction over a damage action arising from the crash of an airplane into Lake Erie: A maritime location was insufficient unless the transaction bore "a significant relationship to traditional maritime activity."

In *Offshore Logistics, Inc. v. Tallentire*,[14] however, the Court upheld admiralty jurisdiction over wrongful-death claims arising from the crash of a helicopter carrying workers from an offshore drilling platform. Not only was jurisdiction "expressly provided" by the Death on the High Seas Act (46 U.S.C. § 461), which covers wrongs "occurring on the high seas beyond a

---

[10]O'Donnell v. Great Lakes Dredge & Dock Co., 318 U.S. 36 (1943).

[11]Warren v. United States, 340 U.S. 523 (1951).

[12]Victory Carriers, Inc. v. Law, 404 U.S. 202 (1971).

[13]409 U.S. 249.

[14]477 U.S. 207 (1986).

marine league from the shore of any state"; jurisdiction also lay under "traditional principles" because the helicopter was "engaging in a function traditionally performed by waterborne vessels." A collision between two pleasure boats is still maritime after *Executive Jet*;[15] an action for injury to shipyard workers exposed to asbestos, according to the courts of appeals, is not.[16]

Admiralty jurisdiction traditionally did not include authority to grant such equitable relief as specific performance or injunctions. Yet the Supreme Court has upheld Congress's power to authorize equitable remedies in admiralty, and in the *Swift* case[17] it sustained the right of a federal court to grant nonstatutory equitable relief that was ancillary to a maritime claim. The subsequent merger of law and admiralty under the Federal Rules of Civil Procedure has helped the lower courts to break down this archaic limitation still further.

Despite § 1333's provision purporting to make federal jurisdiction "exclusive" in admiralty cases, in most instances state courts have concurrent jurisdiction under the ensuing clause "saving to suitors other remedies to which

---

[15]Foremost Ins. Co. v. Richardson, 457 U.S. 668 (1982).

[16]E.g., Oman v. Johns-Manville Corp., 764 F.2d 224 (4th Cir. 1985).

[17]Swift & Co. Packers v. Compania Colombiana del Caribe, 339 U.S. 684 (1950).

they are otherwise entitled." The most important exceptions are for in rem proceedings, actions for limitation of a shipowner's liability, and suits against the United States.

Since most maritime cases are governed by federal law, the question has arisen whether they are also actions arising under federal law within the meaning of 28 U.S.C. § 1331. One might think the question immaterial; the federal court has jurisdiction in any event under § 1333. The right to jury trial, however, may depend upon whether the action can be brought under § 1331, since (except under the Great Lakes Act) there is no jury in admiralty. Seamen seeking damages for personal injury, therefore, tended to join negligence claims under the Jones Act with claims for unseaworthiness and maintenance and cure under the general maritime law and to argue that the entire case arose under federal law.

*Romero v. International Terminal Operating Co.*[18] held it did not. Federal-question jurisdiction, the Court reasoned, had been conferred in order to provide a forum for the vindication of federal rights that had not existed before; § 1333 had already provided a federal forum for claims under the general maritime law. As Justice Brennan observed in a separate opinion, however, this argument proves too much. For a

---

[18]358 U.S. 354 (1959).

maritime case can be filed under § 1332 if the
parties are from different states; since admiralty jurisdiction overlaps with diversity, there
is no reason why it cannot overlap with federal-
question jurisdiction as well.

Though the Court in *Romero* concluded that
jurisdiction over the unseaworthiness and
maintenance claims did not lie under § 1331, it
did not dismiss them, for jurisdiction under §
1333 was plain. Nor did the Court deny the
plaintiff in such a case the right to jury trial on
those claims. Since there was a right to such a
trial on the statutory Jones Act claim (which
*Romero* had inconsistently conceded arose
under federal law), the Court later explained,
and since all three claims arose out of the same
transaction, trial convenience required that they
all be submitted to the jury.[19]

In cases in which there is no Jones Act count to
which claims under general maritime law can
be appended, the issue of § 1331 jurisdiction will
still determine the right to a jury. In some cases,
moreover, it may determine whether a federal
forum is available at all. In *Khedivial Line v.
Seafarers' Int'l Union*,[20] for example, the Second
Circuit refused jurisdiction over an action to enjoin the picketing of a vessel on navigable waters: *Romero* had held that the general maritime

---

[19]Fitzgerald v. United States Lines, 374 U.S. 16 (1963).
[20]278 F.2d 49 (1960).

law was not a "law[] of the United States" within §
1331, and an injunction was not available in admiralty. The Ninth Circuit disagreed, concluding that *Romero* had held only actions that fell
within § 1333 outside § 1331.[21] The latter interpretation tracks *Romero*'s insistence that
Congress intended to provide a forum for cases
not already within federal authority, but it puts a
severe strain on the words of § 1331, for it requires the court to find that the general maritime
law sometimes is and sometimes is not a "law[ ]
of the United States."

The *Romero* decision may also affect removal
from the state courts, for despite the broad terms
of the removal statute ("any civil action") the
lower courts have generally held, in accord with
a dictum in *Romero*, that there can be no removal
if jurisdiction is based solely on § 1333.

---

[21]Marine Cooks & Stewards v. Panama S.S. Co., 265 F.2d
780 (1959).

# IV. Diversity Cases

Article III extends the federal judicial power to "controversies between citizens of different states" or between state citizens and "citizens or subjects" of "foreign states." Federal trial courts have been authorized to hear many such "diversity of citizenship" cases since 1789.

The present statute, 28 U.S.C. § 1332, gives the district courts jurisdiction of diversity cases in which the matter in controversy exceeds $75,000. Similar cases filed in state courts may be removed to federal court under § 1441, but only if no defendant is a citizen of the state in which the suit is filed. The theory is that only an out-of-state litigant has need for the unbiased forum that the diversity jurisdiction was designed to provide. To avoid an inefficient game of musical chairs, however, a local *plaintiff* may file a diversity case in her own federal court.

Many thoughtful observers have argued that there is no longer a significant risk that state courts will discriminate against out-of-state parties, and bills have repeatedly been introduced to limit the jurisdiction to interpleader cases and those involving foreigners, in which it serves additional purposes. Despite pressures engendered by mounting federal dockets, these suggestions have so far fallen on deaf ears.

## A. DETERMINING CITIZENSHIP

State citizenship for diversity purposes means domicile, not residence as the first clause of the Fourteenth Amendment suggests. A change of domicile requires not only a change of residence, the Court has said, but also an intention to make the new residence one's home. On the basis of this test one court held the union leader John L. Lewis to be a citizen of Illinois because his heart was still there, though he had lived in Virginia for thirty years.[1] Determining the citizenship of students, soldiers, and jailbirds presents similar difficulties under this test.

The test of *foreign* citizenship under the diversity clause, on the other hand, has generally been not domicile but nationality. Thus a citizen of the United States who is domiciled abroad is a citizen neither of a state nor of a foreign state and thus, despite the arguable risk of bias, not within the diversity jurisdiction at all.[2] For the reason for federal jurisdiction when foreign citizens are parties, as a lower court had said in a similar case, was to avoid the possibility that state courts might give offense to foreign countries by rendering decisions adverse to their cit-

---

[1] Lewis v. Splashdam By-Products Corp., 233 F. Supp. 47 (W.D. Va. 1964).

[2] Newman-Green, Inc. v. Alfonzo-Larrain, 490 U.S. 826 (1989).

izens – a policy not applicable to the case of an American citizen living abroad.

Diversity jurisdiction does not lie in a suit between two foreigners, even if they are citizens of different countries. The 1789 statute provided for jurisdiction in "all" cases in which an alien was a party, but the Supreme Court construed that language narrowly in order to preserve its constitutionality: Unless the opposing party is a citizen of one of the United States, the case is not within Article III.[3] Section 1330's provision for jurisdiction over "any nonjury civil action against a foreign state" was upheld not on diversity grounds but on the basis that sovereign immunity and its exceptions were governed by federal law;[4] and the recent amendment deeming certain resident aliens citizens of a state (28 U.S.C. § 1332(a)(4)) was intended to reduce rather than to enlarge jurisdiction.

Jurisdiction is determined at the time the suit is filed; a later change of domicile that destroys diversity does not defeat jurisdiction already attached.[5]

In cases brought by or against administrators or executors the Court looked for many years to the citizenship of the representative, not that of

---

[3]Mossman v. Higginson, 4 U.S. 12 (1800).
[4]Verlinden B.V. v. Central Bank of Nigeria, 461 U.S. 480 (1983).
[5]Mollan v. Torrance, 22 U.S. 537 (1824).

the decedent or of his beneficiaries.[6] The opportunity afforded by these decisions for manufacturing or avoiding diversity jurisdiction did not escape the bar. Even in the absence of collusion the citizenship of a representative with no personal stake in the litigation seems unlikely to affect the probability of state-court bias, and § 1332(c) was accordingly amended to make the citizenship of the decedent determinative.

The problem of fraudulent creation of jurisdiction is not limited to cases of administrators and executors. Congress addressed it directly in § 1359, which denies jurisdiction whenever "any party, by assignment or otherwise, has been improperly or collusively made or joined to invoke the jurisdiction" of the federal court.

In an early case the Court refused to hold "improper" the rechartering of a Kentucky corporation in Tennessee though the sole purpose had been to create diversity.[7] Later, in refusing to honor the assignment of a portion of a claim essentially for collection purposes, the Court distinguished *Black & White*: In that case the transfer, whatever its motive, had been absolute.[8] Section 1359 fails to prohibit collusive arrangements to *defeat* jurisdiction, which the

---

[6]E.g., Chappedelaine v. Dechenaux, 8 U.S. 306 (1808).

[7]Black & White Taxicab & Transfer Co. v. Brown & Yellow Taxicab & Transfer Co., 276 U.S. 518 (1928).

[8]Kramer v. Caribbean Mills, Inc., 394 U.S. 823 (1969).

Supreme Court had allowed in *Mecom v. Fitzsimmons Drilling Co.* in 1931;[9] and its language suggests it does not alter the traditional rule that one may move from one state to another for the purpose of creating diversity.[10]

## B. COMPLETE DIVERSITY

### 1. The General Rule

The plaintiffs in *Strawbridge v. Curtiss*[11] were citizens of Massachusetts. So were the defendants, except for one alleged to be a citizen of Vermont. Jurisdiction was denied because diversity was not complete; there were Massachusetts parties on both sides of the case.

The statute does not compel this conclusion, and the Court gave no reasons. Later commentators have suggested that in such a case there is no danger of bias and thus no necessity for federal jurisdiction. In *Strawbridge* itself, where the interests were joint and the suit was filed in the state whose citizens were on both sides, this assumption makes sense: A Massachusetts court could not injure the Vermont defendant without also hurting its own citizens as well.

---

[9]284 U.S. 183.
[10]Williamson v. Osenton, 232 U.S. 619 (1914).
[11]7 U.S. 267 (1806).

If the suit had been brought in Vermont, however, the argument would have been less persuasive: A Vermont jury might well decide for the local defendant even though in so doing it would also have benefited an out-of-state party. Even in the state of common citizenship, moreover, the policy of *Strawbridge* is inapplicable if the interests are several rather than joint. If it is alleged that Massachusetts and Vermont drivers were both negligent, the presence of a local defendant affords no protection to the outsider; the court may find that the latter alone was at fault. *Strawbridge* reserved the question whether in such a case complete diversity would be required, but later cases have uncritically extended the rule. Regardless of the forum, and whether the interests are joint or several, all plaintiffs must be diverse from all defendants to satisfy § 1332.

## 2. Interpleader

Section 1335, however, dispenses with the complete-diversity requirement in interpleader cases, in which a stakeholder sues to determine which of two or more claimants is entitled to property in his possession. To avoid the danger of multiple liability, a stakeholder uncertain whether to pay A or B may wash his hands of the matter by depositing the money in court and leaving the claimants to fight it out for themselves. As the Supreme Court held in *Treinies v. Sunshine Mining Co.*[12] the statutory requirement is only that the *claimants* be "of diverse citizenship;" the citizenship of the stakeholder is immaterial. Thus a Washington stakeholder was allowed to interplead two sets of claimants, one from Washington and the other from Idaho. In *State Farm Fire & Cas. Co. v. Tashire*[13] the Court added that it was not necessary even that there be complete diversity among the claimants themselves: it sufficed that any two opposing claimants were of diverse citizenship.

Although the language of §§ 1332 and 1335 is similar, this discrepancy in interpretation seems justified. The purpose of the interpleader provision was to provide a forum for cases in which due-process limitations on service of process deprived any state court of power to resolve the entire controversy, and that may happen whenever there are two or more claimants from different states.

Since the interpleader statute requires diversity among claimants, it provides no basis for jurisdiction when, for example, a New York stakeholder is confronted by multiple claimants from Pennsylvania. The Second Circuit, however, upheld jurisdiction of such a case under §

---

[12]308 U.S. 66 (1939).
[13]386 U.S. 523 (1967).

1332, the general diversity statute, because the plaintiff was diverse to all the defendants.[14]

There is language in the *Treinies* opinion that casts doubt on this decision, for in upholding the constitutionality of § 1335 the Court appeared to suggest that there was no controversy between the claimants and the "disinterested" stakeholder. If that is true, jurisdiction cannot lie under § 1332. Realistically, however, the stakeholder has a controversy with each claimant which in the absence of relief may result in his having to pay every one of them; it is only after he has deposited the money in court that he loses his stake in the case.

A better explanation for upholding the Interpleader Act is that, as the Court later held in *Tashire*, the *Strawbridge* rule – like the *Mottley* rule in the federal-question field – is not of constitutional dimension. *Kraft* can thus arguably be justified on the ground that, the plaintiff's controversies with each claimant being properly within federal cognizance, the related controversies among the claimants may also be decided under ordinary principles of supplemental jurisdiction.

---

[14]John Hancock Mutual Life ins. Co. v. Kraft, 200 F.2d 952 (1953).

### 3. Supplemental Jurisdiction

There are other situations in which supplemental jurisdiction has made inroads on the *Strawbridge* rule. The lower courts generally held, for example, that a third party might be impleaded under Rule 14 to indemnify the defendant from possible liability, even if the third party was of the same citizenship as the plaintiff or the defendant. However, in *Owen Equipment & Erection Co. v. Kroger*[15] the Supreme Court in such a case refused to permit the plaintiff to make a claim of his own against an impleaded third party from his own state, arguing that otherwise he might evade *Strawbridge* by omitting a logical defendant from his original complaint.

When Congress codified the supplemental-jurisdiction doctrine in § 1367, it took pains to preserve this restriction and added another respecting intervention under Rule 24:

> (b) In any civil action of which the district courts have original jurisdiction founded solely on section 1332 of this title, the district courts shall not have supplemental jurisdiction under subsection (a) over claims by plaintiffs against persons made parties under Rule 14, 19, 20, or 24 of the Federal Rules of Civil Procedure, or over claims by persons proposed to be joined as plaintiffs under Rule 19 of such rules, or seeking

---

[15]437 U.S. 365 (1978).

to intervene as plaintiffs under Rule 24 of such rules, when exercising supplemental jurisdiction over such claims would be inconsistent with the jurisdictional requirements of section 1332.

In *Supreme Tribe of Ben-Hur v. Cauble*[16] the Supreme Court held that in class actions (now governed by Rule 23 of the Federal Rules) jurisdiction depended upon the citizenship of the named representatives, not of other members of the class. Supplemental jurisdiction in such a case would seem to contradict *Strawbridge*; the best explanation may be that absent members, like beneficiaries of an estate, were not considered parties because they could not affect the risk of bias in state court. The meticulous reader will notice that § 1367(b) does not disturb the *Ben-Hur* decision.

There is an obvious tension between *Strawbridge* and the policy against multiple litigation that underlies both supplemental jurisdiction and the federal rules. The complete-diversity requirement forces litigants either to bring their suits piecemeal or to sue in state courts. The disinterested observer may well ask whether the game is worth the candle.

---

[16]255 U.S. 356 (1921).

## C. CORPORATIONS AND ASSOCIATIONS

## 1. Associations as Citizens

Initially the Supreme Court held that corporations were not citizens for purposes of diversity. The consequence was that a corporation could sue or be sued under the diversity clause only if the persons who composed it were diverse to all opposing parties – a rather severe limitation on jurisdiction. Toward the middle of the 19th century the Court changed its tune, ultimately explaining that the "representatives" of the corporation were conclusively "deemed" to be citizens of the state of incorporation – which, of course, in many cases, they were not. *Marshall v. Baltimore & O. R.R.* (1853).[17]

The Court gave two reasons for its conclusion. First, a corporation had essentially the same legal powers as an individual. It could sue, it could be sued, it could make contracts; it therefore should be treated as a citizen for diversity purposes although it was not one under the Privileges and Immunities Clause of Article IV. The second reason was tied to the purpose underlying diversity jurisdiction: A corporation, like an individual, could be the victim or beneficiary of local bias.

---

[17]57 U.S. 314.

In *Chapman v. Barney,*[18] however, the Court put an abrupt end to the growth of this principle, holding without further explanation that a joint stock association, though it resembled a corporation in most relevant ways, was not to be deemed a citizen because it was not a corporation. Similarly, in the *Bouligny*[19] and *Carden*[20] cases the Court reaffirmed *Chapman*'s conclusion that further extensions were for Congress, holding that neither labor unions nor limited partnerships were "citizens" and pointing (in *Bouligny*) to the lack of any obvious test for determining the citizenship of a union that operated in more than one state.

The conclusion that an association is not itself a "citizen" for diversity purposes, however, does not automatically mean that every member of the association must be of different citizenship from the opposing parties. In the *Marshall* case (supra) the Court had presumed the citizenship not of the shareholders but of the officers and directors who represented them. The Second Circuit accordingly held the citizenship of limited partners irrelevant in determining diversity on the ground that the only proper parties were the general partners who had control of the busi-

---

[18]129 U.S. 677 (1889).
[19]United Steelworkers v. R.H. Bouligny, Inc., 382 U.S. 145 (1965).
[20]Carden v. Arkoma Associates, 494 U.S. 185 (1990).

ness.[21] Subsequently the Supreme Court in *Navarro Savings Ass'n v. Lee*[22] held the citizenship of a business trustee rather than of the beneficiaries determinative, over a dissent arguing that the latter had such a degree of control that they should be treated as partners. Nevertheless the Supreme Court in *Carden* rejected the Second Circuit's position, holding that the citizenship of all partners must be considered when a limited partnership was a party. "*Navarro*," the Court said unconvincingly, "had nothing to do with the citizenship of the 'trust,' since it was a suit by the trustees in their own names."

## 2. Determining Corporate Citizenship

For about a hundred years a corporation was considered a citizen only of its state of incorporation. But the place of incorporation often bears little relation to the need for a federal forum, since many corporations doing business in one state incorporate elsewhere to take advantage of favorable tax or corporation laws. Thinking it unlikely that a New York court would discriminate against a Delaware corporation doing all its business in New York, Congress in 1958 required that a corporations be deemed a citizen not only of any state in which it were incorporated,

---

[21]Colonial Realty Corp. v. Bache & Co., 358 F.2d 178 (1966).

[22]446 U.S. 448(1980).

but also of the state in which it had its "principal place of business" (28 U.S.C. § 1332(c)).

This provision works well for corporations doing business in a single state. It does not work so well for United States Steel or Sears Roebuck. Nevertheless a coherent pattern has emerged in the lower courts for determining the citizenship of corporations that do business in more than one state. If, for example, a manufacturing corporation has its plant in one state and its offices in another, the courts are likely to find the principal place of business to be where the factory is situated. On the other hand, if manufacturing plants are scattered among several states and offices are consolidated, the so-called "nerve center" is likely to be found the principal place of business.

### 3. The Consequence of Multiple Citizenship

Section 1332(c) makes many corporations citizens of more than one state but says nothing about the consequences of dual citizenship. Although the 1958 amendment multiplied the occasions for multiple citizenship, the Supreme Court had already had numerous opportunities to determine the diversity effect of incorporation in more than one state, and it had given at least three inconsistent answers to the question.

The predominant view that developed in the lower courts was that jurisdiction depended on the forum: A Pennsylvania plaintiff could sue a Pennsylvania and Delaware corporation in Delaware but not in Pennsylvania. The origin of this rule was the doctrine that the incorporation laws of each state applied only within its borders; in Pennsylvania the dual corporation was a citizen only of Pennsylvania. Diversity policy suggests a more functional rationale: While Pennsylvania incorporation may protect such a defendant from bias in that state, a Delaware court may be tempted to favor its own corporation at the expense of an outside plaintiff. The Third Circuit thought this distinction arbitrary and held a multistate corporation diverse to everybody in any court.[23] The Supreme Court, affirming without opinion a denial of jurisdiction based on the forum rule, made clear this decision was wrong, but it said nothing else to clarify the uncertain law.[24]

It was in this posture that Congress enacted § 1332(c), which created dual citizenship based on a corporation's principal place of business. It is clear that the Third Circuit's view is not the law under this provision. Legislative history made clear that the principal-place-of-business amendment was designed to reduce federal jurisdiction; its effect cannot be to make corporations diverse to everybody in every court.

---

[23]Gavin v. Hudson & Manhattan R.R., 185 F.2d 104 (1950).
[24]Jacobson v. New York, N.H. & H. R.R., 346 U.S. 895 (1953).

Beyond this, the lower courts have generally relied upon the statute's policy of reducing jurisdiction to hold the forum rule inapplicable at least to cases in which citizenship is based upon principal place of business: By analogy to *Strawbridge*, a Pennsylvania plaintiff may not sue a Pennsylvania and Delaware corporation anywhere. An occasional court has held the forum rule nevertheless survives with respect to multiple incorporations, though the distinction makes no sense in policy.

### 4. Derivative Suits

Shareholders' derivative actions have posed difficult problems under § 1332. In a derivative suit a shareholder complains that his corporation has failed to sue a third party who allegedly has done it wrong. The shareholder is a plaintiff and the third party a defendant; the problem is the proper alignment of the corporation on whose behalf the shareholder sues.

Nominally the corporation is a defendant. Moreover, in one sense its interest is opposed to that of the plaintiff, for its refusal to sue the third party is a prerequisite to shareholder litigation. On the other hand, the plaintiff seeks no relief from her corporation, and the corporation will be the beneficiary if she wins.

In early cases the Supreme Court said the corporation should be treated as a plaintiff unless it was "disabled from protecting itself" in that "the very individuals who have a stranglehold over the corporation are the people against whom suit is sought to be brought." The Court abandoned this test in *Smith v. Sperling*[25] in 1957, complaining that its application would make jurisdiction turn on the merits. Rather, said the Court in a companion case, the corporation should be deemed a defendant whenever it is "definitely and distinctly opposed to the institution of . . . litigation." Because the shareholder cannot sue unless the corporation refuses to do so, this may mean always. As the dissenters observed, this rule facilitates the manufacture of diversity cases, since most corporations can find some shareholder who is diverse both to them and to the ultimate defendants.

In terms of diversity policy, the question should be whether the presence of a corporation from the same state as the shareholder on the one hand or the ultimate defendants on the other is likely to have any effect on the sympathies of the triers of fact. Perhaps it is relevant whether the corporation comes into court and argues: If a local corporation tells the jury that other defendants are in the right, a jury may be induced to consider their case favorably. But to make alignment depend upon the position the corporation takes at trial would mean jurisdiction could be determined only after

---

[25]354 U.S. 91.

lengthy proceedings had already been conducted, and the result could be a significant waste of resources. An alternative might be to ignore the corporation, as the stakeholder is ignored in statutory interpleader, and to treat the case as if it were simply a controversy between the shareholder plaintiffs and the third parties. The propriety of such an approach, however, depends upon the assumption that the citizenship of the corporation is unlikely to affect the biases of the trier of fact.

## D. THE JURISDICTIONAL AMOUNT

Ever since 1789 the diversity jurisdiction has extended only to cases in which the matter in controversy exceeds a prescribed minimum value. Five hundred dollars was the original magic number; it has since been raised in stages to $75,000. The purpose of the requirement, according to a Senate Committee in 1958, is to keep the federal courts from frittering away their time on "petty controversies."

For many years the same limitation applied to federal-question cases, with exceptions that gave rise to considerable litigation. In 1980, however, the amount requirement was repealed for virtually all federal-question cases; it continues to apply in diversity.

## 1. Determining the Amount in Controversy

In damage cases the amount in controversy is usually whatever the plaintiff asks, because she may get it from the jury. The claim, however, must be made in "good faith," and jurisdiction will be denied if the complaint shows "to a legal certainty" that the plaintiff cannot recover the minimum the statute requires.[26] Some courts, applying this test, allow dismissal if the judge determines that a verdict greater than the minimum would have to be set aside as excessive; others, fearing (I think unnecessarily) for the right to jury trial, disagree.

More difficult problems of determining the amount in controversy arise when the action is not for damages. For example, in *Healy v. Ratta*[27] the plaintiff sought to enjoin enforcement of a license tax. The Court held the amount in controversy was neither the value of the business nor the penalty for failure to pay, but the lesser amount of the tax, "since payment of it would avoid the penalty and end the dispute." Moreover, the Court refused to consider the capitalized value of the tax over a period of years, because it was not certain that the plaintiff would be in business the following year or that the state would levy the same tax. In contrast, *Aetna Cas. & Sur. Co. v. Flowers*[28] held that future

---

[26]St. Paul Mercury Indemnity Co. v. Red Cab Co., 303 U.S. 283 (1938); Bell v. Preferred Life Assurance Society, 320 U.S. 238 (1943).

[27]292 U.S. 263 (1934).

[28]330 U.S. 464 (1947).

installments were in issue in a workers' compensation action even though they might be cut off by the widow's death or remarriage; and *Healy* distinguished decisions concerning "the validity of a permanent exemption by contract from an annual property tax," although future liability in those cases appeared subject to the same contingencies as future tax liability was in *Healy* itself.

Additional difficulties arise in injunction cases in which it is alleged that one party has more at stake than the other. In *Glenwood Light & Water Co. v. Mutual Light, Heat & Power Co.*,[29] for example, it was argued that the defendant could remove telegraph wires that interfered with the plaintiff's property for $500; the Court nevertheless upheld jurisdiction because the plaintiff alleged they caused it injury in excess of the then applicable minimum of $2,000. *Mississippi & Mo. R.R. v. Ward*[30] suggested without quite deciding that jurisdiction also lay in the converse situation where the plaintiff had less than the amount at stake and the defendant had more. There is no obviously correct answer to this issue, but it would be helpful to have it resolved.

---

[29]239 U.S. 121 (1915).
[30]67 U.S. 485 (1863).

## 2. Multiple Claims

Commentators generally agree that claims by a single plaintiff against a single defendant may always be aggregated for purposes of determining the jurisdictional amount. Aggregation makes perfect sense when one claim exceeds the required amount and the smaller claim arises from the same transaction; judicial economy requires supplemental jurisdiction over the undersized claim. The Supreme Court has also allowed aggregation when neither claim is independently cognizable, though the justification is less apparent. It is difficult to find support in either decisions or policy, however, for allowing aggregation when the claims are unrelated and there is no argument of convenience. The best justification for a flat rule is that its simplicity reduces litigation.

When there are multiple parties, however, the Supreme Court permits aggregation only when the parties have a "common undivided interest" or a "single title or right." Thus claims often cannot be aggregated even if they arise out of a single transaction. While joint owners may aggregate their interests in a suit on a single bond,[31] employees claiming seniority under a single contract may not.[32]

---

[31]Green County v. Thomas's Executors, 211 U.S. 598 (1909).

[32]Thomson v. Gaskill, 315 U.S. 442 (1942).

In *Snyder v. Harris*[33] the Court applied this rule to hold that, despite amendments to F.R.C.P. 23 designed to eliminate distinctions between true and spurious class actions, the refund claims of a class of public-utility customers could not be aggregated because the customers did not share a single undivided interest. The dissenters argued that the judgment would dispose of the interests of all class members, but as the Court observed that had been equally true in cases of voluntary joinder, in which aggregation had been denied. The reasons for the Court's narrow construction, particularly in light of its contrary view when there are only two parties, have not been satisfactorily spelled out; and *Snyder*, while fully in accord with precedent, seriously impairs the effectiveness of the federal class action.

*Snyder* was carried a giant step further in *Zahn v. International Paper Co.*[34] in 1973. Each of the named plaintiffs in *Zahn* alleged a claim that satisfied the amount requirement, yet the Court refused to entertain the claims of other class members that did not independently suffice. While there was one elderly precedent for this conclusion, the dissenters persuasively argued that decisions recognizing supplemental jurisdiction over non-federal claims and impleaded third parties had destroyed its

---

[33]394 U.S. 332 (1969).
[34]414 U.S. 291.

precedential value, and that judicial convenience required that the court take jurisdiction of the entire civil action.

The lower courts have divided on the question whether § 1367 now authorizes supplemental jurisdiction over claims that fail to satisfy the jurisdictional amount. The better view is that it does. Section 1367(a) empowers the court to entertain related claims by or against additional parties whenever it has original jurisdiction over the action itself, as it had in *Zahn*. The limitation in § 1367(b) conspicuously fails to mention class actions or other cases in which there are multiple plaintiffs, and although in other situations it forbids any joinder "inconsistent with the jurisdictional requirements of section 1332" its stated purpose was to forestall evasion of the complete-diversity rule. The House Report on § 1367 does say the new statute was not meant to disturb the result in *Zahn*, but legislative history that contradicts both the language and the purpose of the law is hardly entitled to conclusive weight.

# V. MISCELLANEOUS JURIS-
# DICTIONAL ISSUES

## A. RAISING JURISDICTIONAL QUESTIONS

Questions of subject-matter jurisdiction, such as the absence of diversity or of a federal question, may be raised at any time during trial or appeal, by the court on its own motion, and even by the party who invoked federal jurisdiction to begin with. In the *Mottley* case (supra p. xx) this practice provoked the dismissal, for want of an initial federal claim, of a case in which two important federal questions had been argued and decided below.

The wastefulness of such a rule is apparent, and proposals have been made to change it, such as by forbidding the raising of jurisdictional questions after trial has begun. The Court itself has placed a limit on the doctrine, refusing on obvious grounds of repose to allow a judgment to be attacked collaterally for lack of diversity.[1] Moreover, such objections as venue and service of process must be made early or lost, for, as the Court said in connection with venue, they relate merely to "the convenience of litigants."

Subject-matter limitations on federal jurisdiction, on the other hand, serve interests other than those of the parties: Federalism and the

---

[1]McCormick v. Sullivant, 23 U.S. 192 (1825).

reduction of federal dockets. The parties cannot
be permitted to frustrate those interests by
agreeing to litigate the case in federal court.
Consequently it seems appropriate to allow the
court at some point early in the case to raise such
questions on its own motion; but the decisions
allowing them to be raised throughout the
proceedings arguably carry a good principle too
far.

## B. EXCLUSIVE JURISDICTION

In most cases federal jurisdiction is not exclusive; state courts generally have concurrent
authority. Federal jurisdiction is exclusive,
however, in criminal, antitrust, bankruptcy,
patent, and copyright cases, as well as in suits
against the United States, and in a limited
number of admiralty matters, as noted in
chapter x.

The Supreme Court has drawn some rather
fine distinctions in administering § 1338(a)'s
provision for exclusive federal jurisdiction of
cases arising under the patent laws. An action
for patent infringement arises under those laws,
since the statute both forbids infringement and
provides a remedy; federal jurisdiction is exclusive. The same conduct, however, may constitute
breach of a patent license, which is governed by
state law; if the plaintiff so characterizes her

complaint, it cannot be heard in federal court at all.[2]

Moreover, although the validity of a patent is precisely the kind of issue that gave rise to the exclusive federal jurisdiction, it may be litigated in state court if raised as a defense to an action for breach of license; for federal jurisdiction is exclusive only over cases, not questions, arising under the patent laws.[3] Unfortunately, the same arcane criteria define the exclusive authority of the Court of Appeals for the Federal Circuit to review district-court decisions in patent cases under § 1295.

Congress's power to make federal jurisdiction exclusive, derived from Article III and the Necessary and Proper Clause, was upheld in *The Moses Taylor*[4] in 1867.


## C. STATE COURTS AND FEDERAL OFFICERS

The reader may recall that *Marbury v. Madison*[5] held that the Supreme Court could not constitutionally be given original jurisdiction to issue mandamus against federal officers. Indeed *no* federal court outside the District of Columbia had such authority before the enactment of 28

---

[2]Luckett v. Delpark, 270 U.S. 496 (1926).
[3]Pratt v. Paris Gas Light & Coke Co., 168 U.S. 255 (1897).
[4]71 U.S. 411.
[5]5 U.S. 137 (1803).

U.S.C. § 1361 in 1962, and the Supreme Court held that state courts had none either: Since Congress had declined to give mandamus jurisdiction to federal courts, it must have intended to close the state courts to such actions as well.[6]

In holding in *Tarble's Case*[7] in 1872 that state courts similarly lacked authority to entertain petitions for habeas corpus filed by persons in federal custody, the Court relied not on implied exclusivity of the statute conferring federal jurisdiction over such cases but on principles of intergovernmental immunity reminiscent of *McCulloch v. Maryland*:[8] "[T]he powers of the National government could not be exercised with energy and efficiency . . . if its acts could be interfered with and controlled for any period by officers or tribunals of another sovereignty."

In so concluding the Court stressed the inadequacy of Supreme Court review to prevent irreparable harm before state-court errors could be corrected. "In the meantime," Justice Field wrote, if the state court had discharged a soldier from federal service, "the mischief would be accomplished." There is no such problem in damage actions, and state courts have been permitted to award damages against federal officers.[9] The Court has also allowed state courts to entertain

---

[6]McClung v. Silliman, 19 U.S. 598 (1821).
[7]80 U.S. 397.
[8]17 U.S. 316 (1819).
[9]Teal v. Felton, 53 U.S. 284 (1851).

both criminal proceedings against federal agents and actions to recover property in their possession, although the justification is less clear. Significant harm to federal interests, in any case, is reduced by 28 U.S.C. § 1442, which authorizes federal agencies and officers to remove to federal court any state-court proceeding arising out of their official duties.

## D. REMOVAL

Although most cases within federal trial-court jurisdiction may also be filed in state court, the defendant ordinarily has an option to remove them to the district court under 28 U.S.C. § 1441(a); defendants as well as plaintiffs have a right to a federal forum. The availability of removal significantly impairs the case for making federal jurisdiction exclusive, although in cases where removal could be expected to be almost automatic (as perhaps when the United States is defendant), exclusive jurisdiction may avoid inefficiency. The power to authorize removal, similarly based on Article III and the Necessary and Proper Clause, was sustained in *The Mayor v. Cooper*[10] in 1868.

Section 1441 applies only to civil cases. Both civil and criminal cases, however, may be removed by federal officers sued for acts done in

---

[10]73 U.S. 247.

the course of their duties under § 1442 and by defendants asserting certain civil-rights claims under § 1443.

Section 1441 contains two important limitations, which have already been discussed. The first is the requirement that the case be within the original jurisdiction of the federal courts. As we saw in connection with the *Mottley* case (supra p. xx), this requirement means there can be no removal on the basis of a federal defense. Second, a case resting solely on diversity may not be removed if any defendant is a citizen of the forum state, because the jurisdiction exists to protect outsiders from possible prejudice.

Section 1445 imposes a further limitation, precluding removal of FELA and workers'-compensation cases, in order to protect an impecunious plaintiff's choice of a more convenient forum.

A final implicit limitation, which Congress abolished by enacting § 1441(e), forbade removal of cases over which federal jurisdiction was exclusive. Such a case obviously belongs in federal court, and the technicality that removal jurisdiction is "derivative" will no longer subject the plaintiff who has erroneously chosen a state court to the risk that the statute of limitations may have run on his claim.

## E. THE OBLIGATION OF STATE COURTS TO PROVIDE A FORUM

The converse of the question whether a state court may entertain a federal claim is whether it may refuse to, and the Supreme Court has sometimes held it may not. The first such case was *Mondou v. New York, N.H. & H. R.R.*[11] in 1912, concluding that because the state court would entertain a comparable action under its own law it could not discriminate against a federal action under the FELA.

Similarly, in *Testa v. Katt*[12] the Court held a state court could not refuse to hear a treble-damage action for violation of federal price-control regulations, despite its invocation of the waning conflict-of-laws principle against enforcement of foreign penal claims. Federal law, the Court said, could not be treated as "foreign."

Congress's power to require state courts to hear federal claims seems never to have been seriously questioned. Having authority to create a substantive right under such powers as the Commerce Clause or the war power, the argument goes, Congress under the Necessary and Proper Clause may require that state courts be open to enforce it. By refusing to require Congress to establish inferior state courts, it is

---

[11]223 U.S. 1.
[12]330 U.S. 386 (1947).

said, the Framers indicated their expectation
that state courts would entertain federal cases.

But it is one thing for the states to cooperate
voluntarily in the enforcement of federal law; it
is quite another to coopt state agencies for federal
purposes against their will. The Supreme Court
has made clear that Congress may not coopt state
legislatures or executives;[13] it is not clear why it
should be able to coopt state courts. To close state
tribunals to federal plaintiffs is not to deny
federal rights; Congress may always provide a
federal forum.

Moreover, that Congress may have power to
open the state courts does not mean it has done so,
and the language of neither the FELA nor the
price-control law suggested that it had: Each
provided in essence only that suit could be
brought in any court of competent jurisdiction.

In any event, the obligation of a state court to
entertain federal cases is not absolute, for the
Court has recognized that forum non conveniens
may be a legitimate excuse.[14] As in determining
whether a state ground of decision is adequate to
bar Supreme Court review of a state-court
judgment (see chapter xx), the question is
whether application of a state policy respecting

---

[13]New York v. United States, 506 U.S. 144 (1992); Printz v.
United States, 521 U.S. 898 (1997).
[14]Missouri ex rel Southern Ry. v. Mayfield, 340 U.S. 1
(1950).

the administration of its courts unreasonably interferes with the enforcement of federal rights. In the case of forum non conveniens, the state has a significant interest in not burdening its courts with litigation that might better be conducted in another forum. Indeed, state procedural policies might well be given greater scope in limiting federal claims than in limiting federal defenses; for the plaintiff whom the state court turns away may generally sue elsewhere, while (except insofar as habeas corpus is available in a criminal case) refusal to hear a federal defense destroys it entirely.

## F. VENUE AND SERVICE OF PROCESS

Once it is ascertained that a case falls within federal jurisdiction, limitations on venue and personal jurisdiction, both based on trial convenience and fairness to the parties, determine in *which* federal court the action may be brought.

The basic venue provision (28 U.S.C. § 1391(a) and (b)) permits suit in any district in which a defendant resides (if all defendants reside in the same state) or in which "a substantial part of the events giving rise to the claim occurred." If there is no such district, an action "founded solely on diversity of citizenship" may be brought wherever "any defendant is subject to personal jurisdiction," other cases wherever "any defendant may be found." The reason for this vestigial discrimination against litigants with federal claims is obscure.

Lower courts divide as to whether "reside[nce]" in the venue statute, like "citizen[ship]" under § 1332, means domicile. Under § 1391(c) a corporate defendant is "deemed to reside in any judicial district in which it is subject to personal jurisdiction." Section 1391(e) makes separate provision for suits against the United States or its officers or agencies, and under § 1391(d) an alien may be sued in any district.

Section 1391 applies only to "civil action[s]" and has been held inapplicable to admiralty cases filed under § 1333; the Federal Rules of Civil Procedure, despite the 1966 merger of law and admiralty, attempt to preserve this distinction. Venue in admiralty cases, according to Moore's treatise, lies wherever the defendant may be validly served or his property attached. Nor does § 1391 apply to actions removed from state courts; under § 1441 such actions are removable, if at all, to the district in which the state court sits.

There are special venue provisions for a number of types of cases (e.g., patents, FELA); the applicability to such statutes of the general definition of corporate residence in § 1391(c) has given rise to some difficulty.[15]

Since venue and personal-jurisdiction restrictions serve substantially identical purposes, it is not clear why it is thought necessary to impose them both. Nevertheless, even when venue is proper, Rule 4(k) of the Federal Rules of Civil Procedure permits service of process in most instances only on persons "who could be subjected to the jurisdiction of a court of general jurisdiction in the state in which the district court is located." Exceptions are made for interpleader cases, for parties impleaded under Rule 14 or indispensable under Rule 19, and for actions in which other statutes permit nationwide service. On federal claims, moreover, if no state court would have jurisdiction, Rule 4(k)(2) permits service wherever the Constitution allows.

## G. FORUM NON CONVENIENS AND TRANSFER

In *Gulf Oil Corp. v. Gilbert*[16] in 1947 the Supreme Court held that a federal court in which venue was proper might nevertheless dismiss an action on the basis of the nonstatutory doctrine of forum non conveniens if it might more appropriately have been brought in another location. But

---

[15]Compare Fourco Glass Co. v. Transmirra Products Corp., 353 U.S. 222 (1957) with Pure Oil v. Suarez, 384 U.S. 202 (1966).

[16]330 U.S. 501.

dismissal was a harsh remedy for choosing an unsuitable forum; if the statute of limitations had run in the meantime, the plaintiff would lose his entire case. For this reason Congress in 1948 enacted § 1404(a), which authorizes a federal district court, "for the convenience of parties and witnesses, in the interest of justice," to "transfer any civil action to any other district or division where it might have been brought." Unlike the general venue statute discussed in the preceding section, § 1404(a) has been held applicable to admiralty cases under § 1333.[17]

But § 1404(a) has spawned interpretive problems. Without discussing the question, the Supreme Court has allowed a *plaintiff* to invoke the transfer provision, although he had already had his choice of forum.[18] *Hoffman v. Blaski*[19] relied on the "might have been brought" language of § 1404(a) to forbid transfer to a district in which venue and service would have been improper, although the defendant's waiver of both objections arguably should have cured the problem. *Van Dusen v. Barrack*[20] held that the same language referred only to "the federal laws delimiting the districts in which such an action 'may be brought,'" not to state laws restricting the capacity of foreign personal representatives to

---

[17]Continental Grain Co. v. Barge FBL-585, 364 U.S. 19 (1960).

[18]Ferens v. John Deere Co., 494 U.S. 516 (1990).

[19]363 U.S. 335 (1960).

[20]376 U.S. 612 (1964).

sue. A separate provision allowing transfer from a district in which venue is improper (28 U.S.C. § 1406(a)) was held to apply even though service of process was faulty too, in view of the statutory purpose of avoiding harsh dismissals based upon erroneous choices of forum.[21]

A more recent statute, 28 U.S.C. § 1407, allows transfer to facilitate consolidation of pretrial matters when related cases are filed in more than one federal forum. Under 28 U.S.C. § 2112, when a single administrative order is attacked in more than one court of appeals, proceedings are consolidated in one of them for decision on the merits. Increasingly, moreover, the courts of appeals have concluded that they have "inherent" authority to transfer cases outside the scope of § 2112.[22] To apply similar reasoning to avoid the apparently deliberate limitations on district-court transfers under §§ 1404 and 1406 would be entirely impermissible. Still more recently, however, Congress in § 1631 empowered both trial and appellate courts to transfer any case of which they lack "jurisdiction" to any federal court in which it "could have been brought"; dismissal for filing in the wrong federal forum should fortunately be rare in the future.

Transfer provisions have been generally ap-plauded as conducing to trial in the most appro-

---

[21]Goldlawr, Inc. v. Heiman, 369 U.S. 463 (1962).
[22]E.g., Georgia-Pacific Corp. v. FPC, 512 F.2d 782 (5th Cir. 1975).

priate forum. They are not without countervailing costs, however, for they impose a new burden of litigation to determine the ideal forum. This burden is increased to the extent that the decision whether or not to transfer is subject to appellate review. The better decisions, conforming to Supreme Court directions as to the general scope of appellate mandamus (see chapter 9), have limited that writ to the review of broad questions of statutory power, refusing to reexamine the exercise of discretion in a particular case.

# VI. THE LAW APPLICABLE IN FEDERAL COURTS

## A. *ERIE*

"The laws of the several states," Congress ordained in 1789, "except where the constitution, treaties or statutes of the United States shall otherwise require or provide, shall be regarded as rules of decision in trials at common law in the courts of the United States in cases where they apply." Expanded to include all "civil actions," this provision is now 28 U.S.C. § 1652, the celebrated Rules of Decision Act.

In the famous 1842 case of *Swift v. Tyson*[1] the Supreme Court, unnaturally by modern standards, construed the word "laws" in this statute to include only statutes and such "local" decisional law as that relating to real estate, leaving the federal courts free to determine for themselves, even in diversity cases, the common law governing such "general" matters as bills of exchange.

The Court abandoned this limitation in 1938 in the equally famous case of *Erie R.R. v. Tompkins*,[2] a diversity action for personal-injury damages against an interstate railroad. Historical research had shown, the Court said, that

---

[1] 41 U.S. 1.
[2] 304 U.S. 64.

"laws" in the Rules of Decision Act had been meant to include the entire common law; the line between "local" and "general" laws had proved hard to administer; the existence of a federal common law applicable only in diversity cases made the law disuniform and discriminated in favor of persons from out of state; litigants had gone to great lengths to manufacture diversity in order to shop for a federal forum and application of the general law. But the decisive consideration, wrote Mr. Justice Brandeis for the Court, was the unconstitutionality of the *Swift* decision: "Congress has no power to declare substantive rules of common law applicable in a State. . . . And no clause in the Constitution purports to confer such a power upon the federal courts."

Given the Court's expansive interpretation of the Commerce Clause, there is no doubt that Congress could prescribe rules of liability for interstate railroads today. But the Commerce Clause gives lawmaking power to Congress, not to the courts. State courts, of course, derive authority to make common law from their authority to decide cases. Grants of jurisdiction in admiralty cases and in suits between state have been held to give federal courts similar authority;[3] *Erie* establishes that the grant of diversity jurisdiction does not.

---

[3]Southern Pacific Co. v. Jensen, 244 U.S. 205 (1917); Texas v. New Jersey, 379 U.S. 674 (1965).

The explanation of this distinction lies in the different purposes the Court has attributed to the various clauses of Article III: While the establishment of a uniform law was apparently one reason for the creation of admiralty jurisdiction, the sole purpose of diversity was to provide an unbiased forum.

Thus *Erie* effectively equates the federal diversity court with the disinterested forum in the interstate conflict of laws. Whether a Texas controversy is decided in Oklahoma for party convenience or in federal court to ensure impartiality, the disinterested forum has no concern with the merits and is forbidden to frustrate the wishes of the interested state. It is this principle of respect for state lawmaking authority, above all, that is embodied in the Rules of Decision Act.

## B. SUBSTANCE AND PROCEDURE

The essence of *Erie*, Justice Frankfurter wrote, was that in diversity cases "the outcome of the litigation should be the same, so far as legal rules determine . . . , as it would be if tried in a State court." Consequently the Court held a federal court must dismiss a diversity case when a state statute of limitations had expired;[4] when a state court had dismissed the same controversy on the basis of a statute denying jurisdiction to

---

[4]Guaranty Trust Co. v. York, 326 U.S. 99 (1945).

enter deficiency judgments;[5] when the plaintiff had failed to designate an agent to receive service of process as state law required;[6] when the plaintiff had failed to post security for costs under state law;[7] and when state law forbade specific performance of an arbitration clause.[8] In the analogous context of interstate conflict of laws a disinterested forum will commonly apply its own statute of limitations on the ground that it is "procedural"; but when the state statute is the shorter the Supreme Court's decision to apply it accords far better with the policy underlying both interstate conflicts and *Erie* – that the disinterested forum ought not to frustrate the policies of an interested state.

The mechanical "outcome" test applied in the cases just noted was refined in *Byrd v. Blue Ridge Rural Electric Cooperative*,[9] in which the Court held federal, not state law determined whether a jury or judge should decide whether or not an injured plaintiff was a statutory "employee" whose sole remedy was workers' compensation. The case could have been decided on the straightforward ground that the Seventh Amendment required a jury determination,[10] but the Supreme Court chose instead to lay down a

---

[5]Angel v. Bullington, 330 U.S. 183 (1947).
[6]Woods v. Interstate Realty Co., 337 U.S. 535 (1949).
[7]Cohen v. Beneficial Loan Corp., 337 U.S. 541 (1949).
[8]Bernhardt v. Polygraphic Co., 350 U.S. 198 (1956).
[9]Bernhardt v. Polygraphic Co., 350 U.S. 198 (1956).
[10]Bernhardt v. Polygraphic Co., 350 U.S. 198 (1956).

new test for choosing between federal and state
laws.

To begin with, said the Court, it was by no
means clear that giving the issue to the jury
would change the outcome of the case. Even if it
did, outcome was not the sole consideration. On
the one hand, despite the lack of federal concern
with the merits of the case, there was a strong
"federal policy favoring jury decision of
disputed fact questions" in federal court. On the
other, the state courts in holding that the issue
was for the judge had enunciated no anti-jury
policy, relying simply on precedents whose
concern was to assure meaningful judicial
review of administrative action.

To put the matter once more in choice-of-law
terms, a forum disinterested in the merits may
have a legitimate interest in the application of
rules relating to the administration of its courts;
and the crux of *Erie* is not identity of outcome but
respect for state policy. Since applying the
federal jury rule would serve federal procedural
interests without frustrating state policy, the
Court applied the federal rule. *Byrd* captures
perfectly the position of the disinterested forum.

## C. THE FEDERAL RULES OF CIVIL PROCEDURE

In *Hanna v. Plumer*[11] the Supreme Court in a diversity case upheld service of process pursuant to Rule 4(d)(1) of the Federal Rules of Civil Procedure, which permits leaving the summons with a responsible person at the defendant's home, despite a state law that required delivery to the defendant himself. Since outcome was not the sole test, said the Court, the same result might well have followed even in the absence of a federal rule.

More significantly, however, the Court held that *Erie* and its progeny did not provide the test of the validity of the Federal Rules. Rule 4(d)(1) came within the Supreme Court's authority under the Rules Enabling Act (28 U.S.C. § 2072) to adopt rules governing "the forms of process, writs, pleadings, and motions, and the practice and procedure of the district courts"; "the constitutional provision for a federal court system (augmented by the Necessary and Proper Clause) carries with it congressional power to make rules governing the practice and pleading in those courts" – including matters which, "though falling within the uncertain area between substance and procedure, are rationally capable of classification as either"; and, of course, in case of conflict federal law prevailed under the Supremacy Clause of Article VI.

---

[11]380 U.S. 460 (1965).

Justice Harlan, concurring on the ground that service at the defendant's home did not seriously offend state policy, protested that the Court's test would allow application of any Rule that a "reasonable man could characterize . . . as 'procedural,' . . . no matter how seriously it frustrated a State's substantive regulation." Commentators have added that the Court gave no independent significance to the Enabling Act's requirement that such rules "shall not abridge, enlarge or modify any substantive right." This provision, Professor Ely has argued, does not simply reinforce the requirement that the rules deal with matters of procedure; it invalidates any procedural rule that unduly infringes the substantive interests of a state.

## D. THE CHOICE AMONG CONFLICTING STATE LAWS

In *Klaxon Co. v. Stentor Elec. Mfg. Co.*[12] the Supreme Court held that in determining which state's substantive law to apply under *Erie* a federal court should follow the choice-of-law rules of the state in which it sat. Otherwise, the Court rightly said, the outcome might depend upon whether the case was filed in federal or state court, and it was just such disuniformity that *Erie* was meant to avoid.

---

[12]313 U.S. 487 (1941).

In eliminating intrastate forum-shopping, as Hart and Wechsler observed, this decision created the potential for shopping among federal courts in different states. But the possibility of interstate forum-shopping existed independently of the federal courts, and the basis of *Erie* was not that diversity jurisdiction should be used to make the law uniform; it was that the existence of that jurisdiction ought not to exacerbate the problem by creating additional disuniformities of its own.

Both *Klaxon* and its critics presuppose the traditional understanding that choice-of-law rules exist independently of the substantive laws whose applicability they determine. A conflicting view given wide currency through the writings of Professor Brainerd Currie, however, treats the applicability of substantive law to cases containing foreign facts as an ordinary exercise in construing statutes and common-law rules in light of their purpose. For example, an old Massachusetts statute limiting the contractual powers of married women was presumably designed to protect Massachusetts women from the consequences of their assumed inexperience in business; because there was no reason to think Massachusetts meant to interfere with the policies that other states might adopt for their own citizens, the argument goes, the statute should not be applied to contracts made by out-of-state women in Massachusetts.

On this view *Klaxon* asked the wrong question; in order to effectuate state interests, as *Erie* demands, the diversity court should separately analyze the interstate reach of the substantive law of each related state.

A difficult problem would arise, however, if the court discovered the laws of two or more states to be truly applicable, for the Currie analysis, finding no acceptable means of resolving a true conflict, advises each interested state to apply its own law. This expedient, unsatisfying at best, is unavailable to a disinterested federal court, which has no law of its own. *Klaxon* may well be the best way out, at least if the forum state is one of those whose law applies, since in such a case the *Klaxon* rule serves both to avoid intrastate forum-shopping and to further the policy of an interested state.

In *Griffin v. McCoach*[13] the Court unblinkingly applied *Klaxon* to an interpleader case, although due-process limitations on state service of process often meant that such an action could not have been brought in the courts of the forum state. It makes no sense in terms of *Klaxon*'s policy against forum-shopping to apply the law of a state in which the action could never have been brought. But if one takes the view that the federal court has no tools with which to choose between the laws of two interested states, *Griffin* may be

---

[13]313 U.S. 498 (1941).

the best solution to an otherwise intractable
problem.

*Van Dusen v. Barrack*[14] posed the question
whether after a change of venue under § 1404(a) a
federal court should follow the choice-of-law
rules of the transferor or of the transferee state.
Given that the action had been properly filed in
the original forum, *Klaxon*'s principle that the
existence of federal jurisdiction should not affect
the outcome rightly led the Court to follow the
choice-of-law rules of the transferor state, which
would presumably have been applied if the case
had not been filed in  federal court.


## E. THE FEDERAL COMMON LAW

Despite the *Erie* decision, pockets of federal
common law still survive. In admiralty cases
and suits between states, as noted earlier in this
chapter, the Court has inferred authority to de-
velop  common  law  from  the  grant  of
jurisdiction. It did the same in actions to enforce
collective-bargaining agreements affecting
commerce under § 301 of the Taft-Hartley Act in
the *Lincoln Mills* case, noted in chapter 2. In
other cases the Court has inferred implicit
damage remedies on behalf of injured parties
from federal statutes imposing duties for their

---

[14]376 U.S. 612 (1964).

protection.[15] One may debate whether particular decisions of this nature accurately reflect congressional purpose, but their theory is entirely consistent with *Erie*.

Similarly traditional explanations may be found for the Court's well-known conclusion in *Clearfield Trust Co. v. United States*[16] that federal law governed the rights and duties of the United States on its commercial paper. Not only was the action brought under a jurisdictional provision (28 U.S.C. § 1345, which gives the District Court cognizance of suits brought by the United States) whose purpose might well be held to include protection of the Government's substantive as well as procedural rights, but as the opinion said "the authority to issue the check had its origin" in federal statutes; the Court plausibly concluded that those statutes implicitly dictated development of a uniform federal common law.

Two later Supreme Court decisions, however, cannot so easily be reconciled with *Erie*. *Banco Nacional v. Sabbatino*[17] held that federal common law governed the application of the "act of state" doctrine, which limited a court's investigation of the validity of a foreign expropriation decree. Since the sole basis of jurisdiction was diversity, the jurisdictional statute could not provide the requisite authority. Moreover, the

---

[15]E.g., J.I. Case Co. v. Borak, 377 U.S. 426 (1964).
[16]318 U.S. 363 (1943).
[17]376 U.S. 398 (1964).

court eschewed reliance on substantive federal
statutes, saying only that they "indirectly" supported the decision. The Court said rather that
such international problems were "uniquely federal"; "the Court did not have rules like the act of
state doctrine in mind when it decided *Erie R.
Co. v. Tompkins*."

*Illinois v. City of Milwaukee*,[18] going beyond
the arguably unique field of foreign affairs, held
that federal common law also governed an action by a state to abate the pollution of interstate
waters. Though the opinion cited several federal
water-pollution statutes, it never said which of
them implicitly authorized the creation of common law. The opinion correctly noted that the
Supreme Court had applied federal common law
in an air-pollution case brought by one state
against another within its original jurisdiction,
but that decision was based upon the broad
purposes of the grant of jurisdiction in suits between states. To hold the same law applicable in
other courts, while faithful to *Erie*'s policy
against forum-shopping, would mean federal
common law governed every private water-
rights dispute between persons living in different states.

The *Milwaukee* decision was later overruled
by statute,[19] but the Court's approach leads one to

---

[18]406 U.S. 91 (1972).
[19]See City of Milwaukee v. Illinois, 451 U.S. 304 (1981).

fear that further inroads may henceforth be made upon the clear provisions of the Rules of Decision Act on vague grounds of federal interest. One court of appeals, for example, held that federal common law governed indemnity or contribution for damages resulting from an airline collision because of the "dominant federal interest" in interstate aviation.[20] Much the same could have been said as to interstate railroads in *Erie* itself.

The new federal common law, unlike the general common law applied in diversity cases before *Erie*, applies in state courts too by virtue of the Supremacy Clause.

A special example of the interplay between federal common law and state law is found in maritime cases, for despite the lawmaking powers of the federal courts state laws have frequently been applied in admiralty. The tests for determining when state laws are preempted in such cases have not, however, been consistent.

It is clear enough that state law may not be applied if it contradicts federal, as in the case of a state statute of frauds that would defeat recovery on a contract recognized by federal law.[21] But the absence of a federal right to recover need not always represent a federal policy that there

---

[20]Kohr v. Allegheny Airlines, 504 F.2d 400 (7th Cir. 1974).
[21]Kossick v. United Fruit Co., 365 U.S. 731 (1961).

shall be no recovery. Thus until the Court
developed a maritime remedy for wrongful
death it permitted state laws to give relief for
deaths caused by the breach of maritime duties.[22]
Inconsistently, in cases decided over forty years
apart the Court permitted the states to impose
duties of care going beyond the federal in cases
of death[23] but not of personal injury.[24] The lapse
of time may account for the difference in result.

The best-known case on state laws in maritime cases is Southern Pacific Co. v. Jensen
(1917),[25] which disallowed application of a state
workers' compensation law on the ground that,
apart from any conflict with specific federal policy, it "interfere[d] with the proper harmony and
uniformity" of the maritime law. The argument
was similar to that of pre-emption by the Commerce Clause, but for reasons never explained it
was carried much further, as *Jensen* itself
showed; for the Commerce Clause was held not to
forbid state workers' compensation for interstate
rail workers.

Confusing distinctions grew up as to which
maritime activities were sufficiently "local" as
to avoid the need for uniformity. In workers'
compensation, which was the principal field of
controversy, the practical problem has been

---

[22]Western Fuel Co. v. Garcia, 257 U.S. 233 (1921).
[23]Hess v. United States, 361 U.S. 314 (1960).
[24]Chelentis v. Luckenbach S.S. Co., 247 U.S. 372 (1918).
[25]244 U.S. 205.

largely solved by the extension of a federal statutory remedy to injuries suffered by maritime workers not only on navigable waters but on adjacent areas such as the pier.[26]

*Jensen*'s uniformity principle has been in decline; later Supreme Court decisions allowed application of state law to so peculiarly maritime a field as marine insurance[27] and to damage caused by oil spills.[28] The attorney with a maritime case, nonetheless, would be well advised to be aware of the problem.

## F. FEDERAL LAW IN STATE COURTS

When substantive federal law is enforced in state courts, a problem roughly the converse of *Erie* is presented: Federal policy may require the application of federal law on certain procedural matters as well. Thus in *Dice v. Akron, Canton & Youngstown R.R.*[29] the Supreme Court held the Federal Employers' Liability Act implicitly required that the issue of fraud in the inducement of a release be decided by a state-court jury, notwithstanding contrary state law: "The right to trial by jury is too substantial a part of the

---

[26]33 U.S.C. § 903.

[27]Wilburn Boat Co. v. Fireman's Fund Ins. Co., 348 U.S. 310 (1955).

[28]Askew v. American Waterways Operators, Inc., 411 U.S. 325 (1973).

[29]342 U.S. 359 (1952).

rights accorded by the Act to permit it to be classified as a mere 'local rule of procedure.'"

The analogy to *Erie* is not perfect, for the state court is not necessarily disinterested, as the federal diversity court is; and the Supremacy Clause directs that in any case of true conflict between federal and state policy the former must prevail. The question therefore becomes one of interpretation: To what degree has Congress required (or does the policy of federal common law require) that state interests in the operation of state courts give way? We have seen the application of these principles in considering the degree to which states are required to entertain actions based on federal law (supra pp. xx-yy); we shall see it again in connection with the adequacy of state procedural grounds asserted to block Supreme Court review of federal questions (supra pp. xx-yy).


## G. SECTION 1983

Numerous statutes create express or implied remedies for the violation of federal rights – from copyright or patent infringement to negligent injuries to the employees of interstate railroads. One such statute, however, deserves special mention, for it has been the principal vehicle for the civil-rights and civil-liberties revolution of the second half of the twentieth century, and knowledge of its provisions is essential to understanding the issues considered in the following chapters. That statute is 42 U.S.C. § 1983, which derives from the Civil Rights Act of 1871. Here it is essentially in full:

> Every person who, under color of any statute, ordinance, regulation, custom, or usage, of any State or Territory or the District of Columbia, subjects, or causes to be subjected, any citizen of the United States or other person within the jurisdiction thereof to the deprivation of any rights, privileges, or immunities secured by the Constitution and laws, shall be liable to the party injured in an action at law, suit in equity, or other proper proceeding for redress. . . .

The first thing to notice about § 1983 is that it neither creates substantive rights nor grants jurisdiction to any court. It provides a right of action to redress the deprivation of rights created by other provisions, in a court of competent jurisdiction. A companion provision now codified as 28 U.S.C. § 1343(3) confers federal jurisdiction in substantially similar terms; § 1983 cases arise under federal law within the meaning of § 1331; and under ordinary interpretive principles state courts may and indeed must entertain actions under § 1983.[30]

Section 1983 provides relief against the deprivation of rights under "the Constitution and laws." Federalism concerns reinforce the natural inference that the laws in question are

---

[30]Howlett v. Rose, 496 U.S. 356 (1990).

federal. Rejecting an argument based upon the narrower language of the companion jurisdictional provision ("any Act of Congress providing for equal rights of citizens of the United States"), the Court in *Maine v. Thiboutot*[31] held that the unqualified reference to "laws" authorized § 1983 actions for the violation of *any* federal law.

*Middlesex County Sewerage Authority v. National Sea Clammers Ass'n*,[32] however, added an important qualification: Statutes like the Federal Water Pollution Control Act, which provide their own "comprehensive enforcement scheme," may implicitly preclude relief under § 1983.

Not every violation of "the Constitution and laws" can be remedied under § 1983, but only those perpetrated "under color of any statute, ordinance, regulation, custom, or usage, of any State or Territory or the District of Columbia." Except when private individuals or federal officers act in concert with state officials, therefore, the statute provides a remedy essentially for state and local infringement of federal rights.

*Monroe v. Pape*[33] (1961) raised the important question whether police officers could be sued under §1983 for a search and seizure that of-

---

[31]48 U.S. 1 (1980).
[32]453 U.S. 1 (1981).
[33]365 U.S. 167.

fended state as well as federal law. The majority
held they could: The statute was intended to
provide a remedy not only where state relief was
inadequate in theory but also when it was unavailable in practice. Justice Frankfurter disagreed: § 1983 was not meant to provide redress
for ordinary state torts.

As Justice Harlan pointed out in a separate
opinion, both arguments missed the mark. On
the one hand, there was no showing that Illinois
courts would refuse in practice the relief that
Illinois law promised in theory. On the other the
case involved no "ordinary tort" but the abuse of
state authority. The Court had already held that
the state might offend the Due Process Clause
when its officer exceeded his authority; the *color
of law*" language suggests that § 1983 was meant
to provide a remedy as broad as the rights it was
enacted to protect.

In the same opinion, however, the Court held
without much discussion that only the offending
officers could be sued; the City of Chicago was not
a "person" against whom a § 1983 action might be
brought. Congress in 1871 had rejected on constitutional grounds an amendment offered by
Senator Sherman that would have made local
governments liable for injuries caused by
private individuals in certain cases; the Court
concluded that Congress would have found a
similar obstacle to municipal liability under §
1983.

As Justice Brennan demonstrated when this aspect of *Monroe* was overruled in *Monell v. Department of Social Services* in 1978,[34] this was a non sequitur. What Congressmen had objected to in 1871 was the imposition of a substantive obligation to control private conduct, which would still be questionable today;[35] federal courts had long afforded remedies against municipalities for violations of preexisting duties imposed by the Contract Clause or state law. Thus there was no reason to give the term "person" an unnaturally narrow interpretation; local governments were indeed "persons" within § 1983.

Yet the *Monell* opinion went on to establish a curious exception of its own to the apparent reach of § 1983. A city could be held responsible only for its own policy decisions, not for abuses on the initiative of individual officers; for the debate on the rejected Sherman amendment showed that Congress believed itself without authority to impose vicarious liability on local governments.

As Brennan himself had demonstrated in the first part of the opinion, Congress had believed nothing of the kind. *All* municipal liability is vicarious; a government, like a private corporation, can act only through its agents. Respondeat

---

[34]436 U.S. 658.
[35]See New York v. United States, 506 U.S. 144 (1992); Printz v. United States, 521 U.S. 898 (1997).

superior was a familiar doctrine by 1871. As
*Monroe* suggested, the Constitution itself made
local governments responsible for the
unauthorized acts of its officers, and there is no
reason to doubt that Congress in enacting § 1983
intended to provide a remedy against them.

The states themselves, however, are another
story. Under the Eleventh Amendment and related doctrines discussed in the following chapter, states are constitutionally immune from suit
in federal court even to recover on federal
claims. Thus Congress would not have believed
it could provide remedies against the states
themselves in 1871. Consequently the Court continued to hold that states were not "persons" under § 1983 even after it surprisingly concluded
that Congress *could* lift their immunity by legislation under § 5 of the Fourteenth Amendment;
for there was no evidence that Congress intended
to do so when it enacted the statute.[36]

In *Aldinger v. Howard*[37] (1976) the Court held
that deficiencies in local-government liability
under § 1983 could not be remedied by appending
to an action against county officers a state-law
claim against the county itself. *Monroe* had held
that a local government was not a "person"
within the statute, and pendent jurisdiction
should not be permitted "to circumvent this ex-

---

[36]Will v. Michigan Department of State Police, 491 U.S.
58 (1989).
    [37]427 U.S. 1.

clusion." This was a patent misinterpretation of the *Monroe* opinion; as the dissenters observed, Congress had rejected the Sherman Amendment not out of hostility to vicarious liability but because of a felt lack of constitutional authority.

By holding that local governments are "persons" after all, *Monell* has removed the necessity for supplemental state-law claims challenging official local policy. But the *Aldinger* problem may arise again if a litigant attempts to assert a state-law claim based on an officer's own decision. Section 1367(a), which now authorizes supplemental jurisdiction over additional parties, contains an exception for cases in which such jurisdiction is "expressly" forbidden by federal statute. Section 1983 is surely not express on this subject; one hopes that § 1367 will be taken to have overruled whatever remained of the unfortunate *Aldinger* decision.

Section 1983 is silent on a number of other important issues as well. It does not say, for example, whether the remedies it creates survive the death of one of the parties, and it contains no statute of limitations. Section 1988 of the same Title, however, provides that when federal law is insufficient to provide "suitable remedies" in civil-rights cases the courts may resort to "the common law, as modified and changed by the constitution and statutes of the state" in which they sit. Although some commentators have doubted that this provision was designed for this purpose, the Court has relied on it to permit application of state survival statutes and other state laws in § 1983 cases.[38]

## H. *Bivens*

Section 1983, as noted, provides remedies in most cases only against state and local officers. In *Bivens v. Six Unknown Named Agents*[39] (1971) the Supreme Court found a way to award damages for constitutional violations against federal officers too.

Justice Brennan's cryptic opinion for the majority did not identify the source of this nonstatutory right of action. Quoting *Marbury v. Madison*'s famous dictum that judicial remedies for injuries are "the very essence of civil liberty," Brennan added only that damages had "historically been regarded as the ordinary remedy for an invasion of personal interests in liberty."

Justice Harlan's concurring opinion was more forthcoming. The Court, he said, had long afforded both nonstatutory damages for violation of federal statutes[40] and nonstatutory equitable relief for violation of the Constitution itself. "If a general grant of jurisdiction [in federal-question cases] . . . is thought adequate to em-

---

[38]427 U.S. 1.
[39]403 U.S. 388.
[40]See J.I. Case Co. v. Borak, supra p. xx.

power a federal court to grant equitable relief," Harlan concluded, "then it seems to me that the same statute is sufficient to empower a federal court to grant a traditional remedy at law."

Although Justice Harlan denied it, *Borak* and similar decisions can best be reconciled with *Erie* as exercises in statutory construction. Moreover, as Harlan's own opinion acknowledged, equitable relief in constitutional cases had been based on an express provision of the Conformity Act leaving remedial matters in equity cases, unlike actions at law, to "the principles, rules and usages which belong to courts of equity" – in other words, to federal judge-made law.

Thus the only answer to Justice Black's dissenting protest that the Court had no authority to create a damage remedy against federal officers is that this remedy, like the comparable one in statutory cases, was implicit in the substantive provision the defendants were alleged to have offended – in this case the Fourth Amendment's ban on unreasonable searches and seizures.

There is language in the Court's opinion that lends support to this interpretation, and later cases holding the *Bivens* remedy applicable to other constitutional rights are certainly consistent with this theory. Thus, the Court said in

*Carlson v. Green*,[41] absent "special factors coun-
selling hesitation in the absence of affirmative
action by Congress," damages would lie for a
constitutional violation unless "Congress has
provided an alternative remedy which it explicitly declared to be a *substitute* for recovery directly under the Constitution and viewed as
equally effective." For unless constitutional
rights "are to become merely precatory," as the
Court put it in *Davis v. Passman*,[42] "litigants
who allege that their own constitutional rights
have been violated . . . must be able to invoke the
existing jurisdiction of the courts."

Before the Supreme Court held in *Monell* that
cities were "persons" subject to suit under § 1983,
some lower courts had employed *Bivens* to fill the
gap, arguing that remedies against local
governments, like those against federal officers,
could be inferred from the Constitution itself.[43]
The First Circuit disagreed: The refusal of
Congress to extend § 1983 itself to local governments was "akin to an explicit
Congressional determination that political
subdivisions are not to be held liable in damages
for violation of constitutional rights."[44]

---

[41]446 U.S. 14 (1980).

[42]442 U.S. 228 (1979).

[43]E.g. Hostrop v. Board of Junior College, 523 F.2d 569 (7th
Cir. 1975).

[44]Kostka v. Hogg, 560 F.2d 37 (1977).

This decision was infected by the same fallacy as the Supreme Court's refusal to exercise supplemental jurisdiction over a local government in a § 1983 case in *Aldinger v. Howard*, on which the First Circuit expressly relied. Congress had no wish to preclude relief against cities or counties; as *Monell* makes clear, the narrow scope of § 1983 is attributable to constitutional qualms, not to affirmative policy. One hopes that so long as the Court adheres to *Monell*'s misguided limits on § 1983 relief lower courts will continue to fill the void with *Bivens* remedies.

# VII. SOVEREIGN IMMUNITY

## A. THE GENERAL PRINCIPLE

In reaction to *Chisholm v. Georgia*[1] (1793), which had held the diversity jurisdiction included an action against one state by a citizen of another, the Eleventh Amendment excludes from federal judicial power "any suit in law or equity" against a state by "citizens of another State, or by Citizens or Subjects of any Foreign State." On the theory that this provision was intended to restore the original understanding of Article III, the Supreme Court has gone beyond the terms of the amendment to hold that the judicial power does not include a suit against a state in admiralty[2] or by a federal corporation.[3] Most important, as the Court concluded in *Hans v. Louisiana*[4] in 1890, it does not extend to by one of its own citizens on the basis of federal law.

Similarly, though the Constitution is silent on the subject, the United States is implicitly immune from suit as well.[5] Municipal corporations, on the other hand, do not share the states' immunity.[6]

---

[1] 2 U.S. 419.
[2] Ex parte New York, 256 U.S. 490 (1911).
[3] Smith v. Reeves, 178 U.S. 436 (1900).
[4] 134 U.S. 1.
[5] Kansas v. United States, 204 U.S. 331 (1907).
[6] Chicot County v. Sherwood, 148 U.S. 529 (1893).

A state is not immune, however, from suit by the United States or by another state, because, the Court said, a federal tribunal to resolve such disputes was the Constitution's substitute for war.[7] This rationale, the Court concluded in *Monaco v. Mississippi*,[8] was inapplicable when a state was sued by a foreign nation. Moreover, *Kansas v. United States*[9] inconsistently held that a state could not sue the United States in federal court, ignoring the argument the Court had so persuasively made in the converse case and saying simply that "public policy forbids."

A dictum in *Monaco* suggested that foreign states enjoyed a comparable constitutional immunity. But Congress in 1976 passed a statute purporting to make foreign states suable in actions "based upon a commercial activity" or a "tortious act or omission" with connections to the United States (28 U.S.C. §§ 1604-05). Thus Congress thought the pre-existing foreign-state immunity was not of constitutional dimension; the House Report traced it to *The Schooner Exchange v. McFaddon*,[10] an 1812 decision construing a statutory jurisdictional grant narrowly in deference to international custom. Yet the argument for a constitutional immunity is similar to that made in any suit against a state outside the Eleventh Amendment. As Hamilton said in

---

[7]United States v. Texas, 143 U.S. 621 (1892).
[8]292 U.S. 313 (1934).
[9]See note 5 supra.
[10]11 U.S. 116.

The Federalist to quiet fears that the Diversity Clause would make states subject to suit in federal court, "[i]t is inherent in the nature of sovereignty not to be amenable to the suit of an individual without its consent."

In 1972 Congress made the anti-discrimination requirements of the 1964 Civil Rights Act applicable to employees of state governments and expressly authorized relief against the state itself for violating its provisions. Numerous decisions had made the obvious point that Congress could not give federal courts jurisdiction of matters outside the federal judicial power as defined by Article III, and *Hans v. Louisiana* had established that suits against states did not fall within that Article. Nevertheless the Supreme Court in *Fitzpatrick v. Bitzer*[11] managed to uphold the statute.

Section 5 of the Fourteenth Amendment, Justice Rehnquist[!] wrote, expressly authorized Congress "to enforce, by appropriate legislation, the provisions of this article"; and the first section of that Amendment expressly embodied "limitations on state authority." Thus, the Court concluded, the Fourteenth Amendment implicitly modified the preexisting doctrine of sovereign immunity, and in order to enforce it Congress could "provide for private suits against States or state officials which are

---

[11]427 U.S. 444 (1976).

constitutionally impermissible in other contexts."

This reasoning is less than overpowering. One might have thought § 5 of the Fourteenth Amendment, like other grants of legislative power, was subject to explicit and implicit constitutional limitations; no one would read it to authorize the imposition of cruel and unusual punishments. That the amendment limits state sovereignty, moreover, does not distinguish it from the Contracts Clause, which the Court had long held limited by sovereign immunity.

In any event, *Fitzpatrick* did not hold that the Fourteenth Amendment of its own force rendered sovereign immunity inapplicable; the decision was based upon the express action of Congress in abrogating immunity under § 5. Thus in the absence of statute the state is still immune even if the case is based upon the Fourteenth Amendment, and the Court has continued to hold that § 1983, which does not expressly authorize suits against states, does not lift their constitutional immunity.

After first deciding the other way without agreeing on a majority opinion,[12] the Court in *Seminole Tribe v. Florida*[13] (1996) held that the Commerce Clause, unlike the Fourteenth

---

[12]Pennsylvania v. Union Gas Co., 491 U.S. 1 (1989).
[13]517 U.S. 44.

Amendment, did not empower Congress to abrogate a state's immunity from suit in federal court. The Court had implied as much in *Fitzpatrick*, and the conclusion seems obvious so long as *Hans v. Louisiana* is law; federal courts cannot be given jurisdiction of matters outside Article III. *Fitzpatrick* itself is hard enough to swallow, but at least the Fourteenth Amendment was enacted after the Constitution and therefore gave rise to a plausible argument of implied repeal.

Thus as the Court understands it the Fourteenth Amendment allows Congress to limit a state's immunity, but the original Constitution does not. Litigants have consequently waxed inventive in their efforts to demonstrate that all sorts of federal statutes traditionally justified in other terms were based in fact on the Fourteenth Amendment, but so far without persuading the Supreme Court. Thus in two 1999 cases the Court appropriately decided that Congress could not make states suable either for unfair competition or for patent infringement in federal court.[14] These decisions seem clearly correct. Whatever "due process of law" may require in such a context, not every official trespass on intellectual property rights is a "deprivation" or

---

[14]College Savings Bank v. Florida Prepaid Post-Secondary Education Bd., 119 S.Ct. xxxx; Florida Prepaid Post-Secondary Education Bd. v. College Savings Bank, 119 S.Ct. yyyy.

"taking" of property within the meaning of the Constitution.

On the same day the Court took a more significant step in the same direction in *Alden v. Maine*,[15] concluding that Congress could not make states suable in *their own* courts for failure to pay their employees wages in accord with the Fair Labor Standards Act. Like most cases upholding sovereign immunity, *Alden* was a 5-4 decision, and it is decidedly unpopular. Yet it too, alas, seems entirely correct. To framers who believed, as Hamilton said, that a state could not be sued without its consent, the notion that Congress could make states suable in their own courts would never have occurred.

Sovereign immunity is not an attractive concept. But implicit constitutional immunities are as old as *McCulloch v. Maryland*.[16] If as the Court has repeatedly held sovereign immunity limits the grants of judicial power in Article III[17] and intergovernmental immunity forbids Congress to coopt state legislative or executive agencies under the Commerce Clause,[18] it makes sense to hold that immunity from suit limits the commerce power as well.

---

[15]119 S.Ct. zzzz.

[16]17 U.S. 316 (1819).

[17]E.g., Hans v. Louisiana, supra.

[18]New York v. United States, 506 U.S. 144 (1992); Printz v. United States, 521 U.S. 898(1997).

## B. WAIVER

Because sovereign immunity exists for the protection of the government, it may be waived at pleasure. The United States has done so in a number of types of cases.

For example, 28 U.S.C. § 1491 gives the Court of Federal Claims jurisdiction of damage actions based on contract or on the Constitution, statutes, or regulations. The Tucker Act, § 1346(a), gives the same jurisdiction to the district courts provided that the amount in controversy is *less* than $10,000.

The Federal Tort Claims Act, 28 U.S.C. § 1346(b), gives the district courts jurisdiction over tort cases against the United States, subject to a number of limitations spelled out in § 2680. Two of the most important exceptions are those for intentional torts (amended not so long ago to allow recovery for certain acts of law-enforcement officers) and for injuries caused in the exercise of "discretionary" functions. The latter exception was generously held in *Dalehite v. United States*[19] to preclude recovery for government negligence in manufacturing and handling nitrate fertilizers that resulted in a legendary explosion in Texas City.

---

[19]346 U.S. 15 (1953).

Apart from these exceptions, the Tort Claims Act permits recovery of damages for injury or death "caused by the negligent or wrongful act or omission" of government employees acting within the scope of their employment, "under circumstances where the United States, if a private person, would be liable to the claimant in accordance with the law of the place where the act or omission occurred." By providing relief only for "wrongful act[s]," the Court unconvincingly concluded,[20] Congress excluded strict liability. By incorporating the law of the state in which the "act or omission" occurred, the Justices just as unconvincingly declared,[21] the statute also departed from not one but two traditional principles of the conflict of laws. It required application of the law of the place of negligence rather than injury, and it required application of the law that a court of that state would apply to a similar case, which did not always mean its own substantive rules.

The Suits in Admiralty Act, 42 U.S.C. § 741, and the Public Vessels Act, 46 U.S.C. § 781, authorize suits against the United States for injuries caused by government vessels. Government employees injured on the job may seek workers' compensation from an administrative agency under 5 U.S.C. § 751. And in 1976 Congress amended the Administrative Proce-

---

[20]Laird v. Nelms, 406 U.S. 797 (1972).
[21]Richards v. United States, 369 U.S. 1 (1962).

dure Act (5 U.S.C. § 702) to provide that a federal-court action "seeking relief other than money damages and stating a claim that an agency or an officer" of the United States "acted or failed to act in an official capacity or under color of legal authority" was not to be barred by sovereign immunity even if the Government was itself made a party.

This is a patchwork system with many gaps in it, representing no coherent policy as to when suits against the government should be allowed, and it is often difficult to determine under which statute a particular claim should be brought.

The interpretation of *state* statutes consenting to suit is of course a matter of state law. A state may consent to be sued only in its own courts, subject to Supreme Court review;[22] and a state provision allowing suit in "any court of competent jurisdiction" has been held to open only state, not federal courts.[23] The importance of immunity has led the Court to hold that it may be raised for the first time on appeal.[24]

In sharp contrast to its general definition of waiver as the "intentional relinquishment of a known right,"[25] the Supreme Court in *Parden v.*

---

[22]Smith v. Reeves, 178 U.S. 436 (1900).

[23]E.g., Kennecott Copper Corp. v. State Tax Comm., 327 U.S. 573 (1946).

[24]Edelman v. Jordan, 415 U.S. 651 (1974).

[25]Johnson v. Zerbst , 304 U.S. 458 (1938).

*Terminal Ry.* in 1964 astoundingly concluded that by operating an interstate railroad Alabama had consented to be sued under the FELA.[26] The Court has since squarely repudiated this untenable doctrine. "Constructive consent," as the Court coldly observed in a 1974 opinion, "is not a doctrine commonly associated with the surrender of constitutional rights"; and whatever remained of *Parden* was formally overruled in 1999.[27] Henceforth, it seems, a state will be found to have consented to suit only if it has actually consented.

## C. SUITS AGAINST GOVERNMENT OFFICERS

Governments, like private corporations, can act only by agents; to enjoin a government official from acting effectively enjoins the government itself. On the other hand, if sovereign immunity were a bar to all injunctions against government officers, the Constitution could not be adequately enforced. Consequently, when a state officer was alleged to have acted unconstitutionally or beyond his statutory authority, the Court invoked the fiction that he was not acting for the state and therefore was not protected by its immunity. *Ex parte Young* (1908).[28] Before the 1976 amendment to the Administrative Pro-

---

[26]377 U.S. 184.
[27]College Savings Bank v. Florida Prepaid Post-Secondary Education Bd., 119 S.Ct. xxxx.
[28]209 U.S. 123.

cedure Act expressly authorizing similar actions against federal officers, the same fiction was applied to them too.

The irony of this fiction is that what is thus held not to be state action for purposes of jurisdiction violates the Constitution only because it *is* state action for purposes of the substantive law.

*Ex parte Young* does not mean that a state officer may *always* be sued on the ground that she is acting beyond her authority. In *Edelman v. Jordan*,[29] for example, the Supreme Court held that sovereign immunity forbade ordering a state officer to make welfare payments out of the state treasury to remedy past violations of federal law. Conceding that *Young* authorized injunctions against future violations, the Court invoked earlier decisions refusing to order tax collectors to pay refunds with public money, concluding that a private suit "seeking to impose a liability which must be paid from public funds in the state treasury" did not come within *Ex parte Young*.

As an original matter there is little to recommend this distinction. In one of the tax cases cited in *Edelman* the Court had said the suit was "in essence" against the state and that the state was the "substantial party in interest," but that was equally true in *Ex parte Young*. As the Court

---

[29]415 U.S. 651.

acknowledged, an injunction permissible under *Young* can have as adverse an impact upon state policy as an order to pay money outlawed by *Edelman*. Indeed in *Edelman* itself it must have cost the state more money to meet federal requirements in all future cases than it would have to pay for three years of past violations.

Nevertheless the *Edelman* decision was fully in accord with longstanding precedent and did not represent a retreat from *Ex parte Young*. Reviewing a long series of prior cases in 1891, the Court divided suits against state officers into two categories. A suit to compel officers "to do acts which constitute a specific performance" of state contracts was forbidden; a suit to preclude "acts of wrong and injury to the rights and property of the plaintiff acquired under a contract" was not.[30] Thus, for example, the Court in *North Carolina v. Temple*[31] (1890) held that immunity precluded a federal court from ordering a state auditor to pay the holder of bonds on which the state had defaulted.

The source of these unsatisfying distinctions was the fiction the Court had utilized to permit suit in such cases as *Ex parte Young*. As the Court explained in *In re Ayers*[32] in 1887, if a state officer is stripped of his authority when he offends the Constitution, he cannot commit a

---

[30]Pennoyer v. McConnaughy, 140 U.S. 1.
[31]134 U.S. 22.
[32]123 U.S. 443.

breach of the state's contract; for only the state is a party to the obligation. On the same reasoning, an officer stripped of his authority could not be responsible for failure to satisfy the state's welfare obligations in *Edelman*. On the other hand, to seize or threaten to seize the plaintiff's property is a tort even if the defendant is stripped of his authority; thus the victim can sue to prevent such action or to recover his property from the official "personally." To put the matter in terms of the traditional law of agency, an agent is liable for torts committed in the scope of his employment, but not for contracts made on behalf of his principal.

By the time of *Edelman* the Court had lost sight of the original reason for these distinctions, and the *Edelman* opinion did not rely directly on *Ayers*. In later cases. moreover, the Court has taken a liberal view of the relief available against a state officer. In *Hutto v. Finney*,[33] for example, the Court not only upheld an award of attorneys' fees to be paid out of state funds on the ground that Congress (in 42 U.S.C. § 1988) had abrogated the state's immunity under *Fitzpatrick v. Bitzer*; it went on to sustain an additional award not covered by that statute on the ground that it was "ancillary" to a prospective injunction and thus permitted by language in *Edelman* – although a close reading of the latter

---

[33]437 U.S. 678 (1978).

opinion reveals that the Court had had something entirely different in mind.

More significant was *Milliken v. Bradley*,[34] where the Court upheld an order requiring the use of state money to provide "compensatory or remedial educational programs for schoolchildren who have been subjected to past acts of *de jure* segregation." This order, the Court said, fit "squarely within the prospective-compliance exception reaffirmed in *Edelman*" because it required the state to set up the remedial program "prospectively." But *all* relief for past wrongs is prospective in that sense; the officer in *Edelman* had been ordered to pay past-due installments in the future. The Court added that in *Milliken* the money was not to be paid to the wronged pupils themselves, but it did not say why that mattered.

In sharp contrast to the permissive attitude displayed in the cases just noted was the 1984 decision in *Pennhurst State School & Hospital v. Halderman*,[35] which essentially held that a state officer could not be sued even for prospective relief on the basis of state law. *Ex parte Young*, Justice Powell explained, had been based on the necessity of "permit[ting] the federal courts to vindicate federal rights"; there was no such necessity "when a plaintiff alleges that a state official has violated state law." Not only was this

---

[34]433 U.S. 267 (1977).
[35]465 U.S. 89.

conclusion, as Justice Stevens demonstrated in dissent, a radical though unacknowledged departure from precedent; whatever the underlying reason for *Ex parte Young*, its theory had been that an officer acting without authority was not the "state" for immunity purposes, and that theory was applicable by definition to officers acting contrary to state law.

In *Seminole Tribe v. Florida*[36] the Court unsurprisingly added that relief under *Ex parte Young*, like an action under § 1983, might implicitly be barred by its omission from a comprehensive statutory scheme for the enforcement of particular federal rights.

Not long after *Pennhurst* the Court built upon its reasoning to suggest a new justification for the distinction between *Young* and *Edelman*:

> Remedies designed to end a continuing violation of federal law are necessary to vindicate the federal interest in assuring the supremacy of that law. . . . But compensatory or deterrence interests are insufficient to overcome the dictates of the Eleventh Amendment.[37]

Despite the Court's efforts, the law of sovereign immunity in suits against state officers remains both confused and difficult to reconcile with rational modern policy. In the case of

---

[36]517 U.S. 44.

[37]Green v. Mansour, 474 U.S. 64, 68 (1985).

federal officers the recent APA amendment is a substantial improvement, but it still authorizes neither "money damages" nor any other relief expressly or impliedly forbidden by other provisions. The Committee Report unexpectedly explains that by authorizing actions for damages in government-contract cases in §§ 1346 and 1491 Congress implicitly precluded suits for specific performance.

## D. OFFICIAL IMMUNITY

Because personal damage or criminal judgments against government officers do not directly impede official functions, sovereign immunity does not bar them.[38] However, because the fear of such judgments may interfere with those functions by deterring officers from vigorous prosecution of their jobs, a separate nonconstitutional doctrine of "official" immunity grew up at common law and has been read into 42 U.S.C. § 1983, which authorizes civil actions against state officers.

In the case of legislators,[39] judges,[40] and prosecutors,[41] the immunity from damages is absolute, lest the burden and risks of litigation itself deter. Other executive officers, however, such as

---

[38]Scheuer v. Rhodes, 416 U.S. 232 (1974).
[39]Tenney v. Brandhove, 341 U.S. 367 (1951).
[40]Pierson v. Ray, 386 U.S. 547 (1967).
[41]Imbler v. Pachtman, 424 U.S. 409 (1976).

governors and policemen, are extended only a limited immunity:[42] They are not liable unless, as the Court said in a related context, their conduct "violate[s] clearly established statutory or constitutional rights of which a reasonable person would have known."[43] The distinction is based upon the nature of the action challenged, not upon the title of the officer; the justices of a state court were accorded an absolute immunity in the "legislative" task of promulgating regulations and a qualified one in the "executive" task of enforcing them.[44]

Official immunity is generally inapplicable to injunctions, which, because they do not deprive the officer of her money or liberty, pose little threat to vigorous performance of her duties.[45] But from legislative actions, where damage immunity is absolute, the official may not be enjoined either.[46] The court below explained that, since the reason immunity was absolute was to spare legislators the burden of litigation, injunction suits against them fell within the policy of the rule. Since no retrospective sanctions are involved, however, the legislator has no personal incentive to defend. To apply the same reasoning to prosecutors, whose damage immunity is

---

[42]Scheuer v. Rhodes, supra note 38.

[43]Harlow v. Fitzgerald, 457 U.S. 800 (1982).

[44]Supreme Court of Virginia v. Consumers Union, 446 U.S. 719 (1980).

[45]Littleton v. Berbling, 468 F.2d 389 (7th Cir. 1972).

[46]*Supreme Court of Virginia*, supra note 44.

also absolute, would set aside a vast body of decisions in which the contrary was assumed; prosecutors are enjoined every day under *Ex parte Young*.

Accordingly, the Court properly concluded in *Pulliam v. Allen*[47] that a judge could be sued for injunction under § 1983, only to go too far in the other direction by holding he could be held personally liable for the plaintiff's attorney's fees – thereby deterring him from performance of his duty as effectively as if he were liable for damages. Moreover, the Court has flatly declared in dictum that even state judges acting in their judicial capacity have no official immunity from criminal liability under federal Civil Rights Acts.[48] Similarly, it has rejected outright the claim that a state legislator is immune from federal bribery prosecution.[49]

Local governments do not share their officers' immunity from damage liability under § 1983. Not only is it "fairer" that the cost of a constitutional violation be "borne by all the taxpayers" than by the innocent victim, but "it is questionable whether the hazard of municipal loss will deter a public officer from the conscientious exercise of his duties."[50]

---

[47] 466 U.S. 522 (1984).

[48]O'Shea v. Littleton, 414 U.S. 488 (1974).

[49]United States v. Gillock, 44 U.S. 360 (1980).

[50]Owen v. City of Independence, 445 U.S. 622 (1980).

Under federal common law that has survived the *Erie* decision, federal executive officers appear to enjoy absolute immunity from damage liability under state defamation law.[51] In *Butz v. Economou*,[52] however, the Court held that a Cabinet officer sued for damages resulting from a violation of the Constitution was qualified only: "There is no basis for according to federal officials a higher degree of immunity from liability when sued for a constitutional infringement as authorized by *Bivens* than is accorded state officials when sued for the identical violation under §1983."

## E. CONGRESSIONAL AND PRESIDENTIAL IMMUNITIES

Members of Congress enjoy two explicit constitutional immunities. First, they are "privileged from arrest" during sessions except in cases of "treason, felony and breach of the peace." This clause has been construed to exempt members only from the obsolete practice of arrest in civil cases, not from service of ordinary civil process or from criminal arrest. More significant is the provision (also in Article I, § 6) that for "any speech or debate in either house" a member "shall not be questioned in any other place." The purpose of this provision, the

---

[51]Barr v. Matteo, 360 U.S. 564 (1959).
[52]438 U.S. 478 (1978).

Supreme Court has said, is to strengthen the independence of Congress.[53]

"Speech or debate" includes all "things generally done in a session of the House . . . in relation to the business before it,"[54] but not contact
with the executive branch on behalf of a con-
stituent[55] or the private publication of material
gathered in a legislative hearing.[56] Despite earlier statements to the contrary, it now seems established that because of the indispensability of
staff assistance congressional aides enjoy the
same immunity as the members themselves.[57]
And in *Eastland v. United Servicemen's Fund*[58]
the Court without discussion held the Speech or
Debate Clause barred injunctive as well as criminal or damage relief, as the Court was later to
hold of the nonconstitutional "official
immunity" of *state* legislators under § 1983.[59]

Unlike members of Congress, Presidents enjoy no explicit constitutional immunity. In
*Nixon v. Fitzgerald*,[60] however, the Court relied
on the President's unique constitutional status to
afford him an implicit absolute immunity from
constitutional damage actions that is shared

---

[53]United States v. Johnson, 383 U.S. 169 (1966).
[54]Kilbourn v. Thompson, 103 U.S. 168 (1881).
[55]United States v. Johnson, supra note 53.
[56]Gravel v. United States, 408 U.S. 606 (1972).
[57]Ibid.
[58]421 U.S. 491 (1975).
[59]*Supreme Court of Virginia* , supra note 44.
[60]457 U.S. 731 (1982).

neither by Cabinet officers[61] nor – in contrast to the immunity of members of Congress under the Speech and Debate Clause – by the President's own assistants.[62]

The Court once held that the President could not be enjoined from enforcing the allegedly unconstitutional reconstruction laws,[63] but there seems no more reason for that than in the analogous case of other executive officers, who can be freely enjoined; the District of Columbia Circuit seems quite right in concluding that the Court would not follow *Mississippi* today.[64] In 1974, indeed, without even discussing the question whether the President was immune from civil process entirely, the Supreme Court in United States v. Nixon[65] upheld a famous court order directing him to produce documentary and taped evidence.

In 1997, indeed, in *Clinton v. Jones*,[66] the Court unanimously rejected the President's contention that the Constitution protected him from being distracted from his duties to defend a tort action for conduct allegedly committed before his election: *Fitzgerald* applied only to actions for wrongs committed in the course of official duty.

---

[61]Butz v. Economou, supra note 52.
[62]Harlow v. Fitzgerald, 457 U.S. 800 (1982).
[63]Mississippi v. Johnson, 71 U.S. 475 (1867).
[64]Nixon v. Sirica, 487 F.2d 700 (1973).
[65]418 U.S. 683.
[66]520 U.S. 681.

Nevertheless there remains a widespread belief
that a sitting President may not be prosecuted for
crime; even the Supreme Court might find it
awkward for him to run the government from the
penitentiary.

# VIII. ABSTENTION AND RELATED DOCTRINES

In 28 U.S.C. §§ 1341 and 1342, on grounds of federalism, Congress forbade federal courts to restrain the enforcement of state taxes, and of many state public-utility rate orders, when state courts provided a "plain, speedy, and efficient remedy." In a number of other cases, without benefit of statutory direction, the Supreme Court has held that federal courts ought not to exercise the jurisdiction that Congress has given them.

## A. *PULLMAN*

In *Railroad Commission v. Pullman Co.*,[1] for example, a state administrative order requiring conductors on all sleeping cars was attacked on grounds of racial discrimination under both federal and state law. Finding the state law unclear and the federal constitutional question substantial, the Supreme Court in an opinion by Justice Frankfurter ordered "abstention": The case should be held pending resort to state court for an interpretation of state law.

Abstention in this context, as the Court said in *Pullman*, serves to prevent three distinct evils: the unnecessary decision of constitutional questions, unnecessary friction between federal

---

[1]312 U.S. 496 (1941).

courts and the states, and the risk of error in determining the meaning of state law.

*Pullman* was an action arising under federal law; the court had jurisdiction under § 1331. The traditional reluctance to decide unnecessary constitutional questions cannot justify the Court's refusal to decide the controversy; constitutional questions are normally avoided by deciding the case on nonconstitutional grounds, not by kicking the parties out of court. Nor can abstention be squared with the statute on the familiar ground that equity does not act when there is an adequate legal remedy. For as Justice Frankfurter himself pointed out in a case in which he thought abstention improper, only a *federal* remedy can be adequate for this purpose; the very premise of federal jurisdiction is that state remedies are inadequate to protect federal rights.

Troubled by the tension between *Pullman* abstention and the jurisdictional statute, the Court set limits to the doctrine in *England v. Louisiana State Board of Medical Examiners*[2] in 1964. Once the federal court abstains, the parties must submit to the state court only questions of state law; they may reserve federal questions for later federal decision.

---

[2]375 U.S. 411.

*England* blunts some of the objections to *Pullman*, but it does not eliminate them entirely. The statute gives jurisdiction over the entire civil action, not merely the federal questions it poses; and when the action is also based on diverse citizenship abstention denies the out-of-state litigant protection from state-court bias in the application of state law. Moreover, at best abstention splits what ought to be a single case between two forums at the expense of judicial economy and significantly delays the vindication of federal rights. In cases in which the propriety of abstention is first discovered on appeal from a federal decision on the merits, the entire process has been known to take ten years.

The paradigm case for *Pullman* abstention is a suit to enjoin a state officer from enforcing ambiguous state law on substantial federal constitutional grounds. *Pullman* has been applied to civil-rights cases under 42 U.S.C. § 1983,[3] despite the mistrust of state courts reflected by that provision and stressed by the Court in arguably analogous cases. Abstention may also be ordered in suits brought by the United States.[4]

Yet abstention is not automatic even when resolution of unclear state law can avoid a substantial constitutional question. In *Pike v. Bruce Church, Inc.*,[5] for example, delay in de-

---

[3]Harrison v. NAACP, 360 U.S. 167 (1959).
[4]Leiter Minerals v. United States, 352 U.S. 220 (1957).
[5]397 U.S. 137 (1970).

termining whether a state statute could
constitutionally be applied to a particular
transaction would have resulted in loss of a
$700,000 crop; abstention was refused "in view of
the emergency situation presented, and the fact
that only a narrow and specific application of the
Act was challenged." Moreover, the Court for no
persuasive reason has held abstention
inappropriate when the unclear state law
"mirrors" a provision (such as the Equal
Protection Clause) of the federal Constitution.[6]

*Pullman* abstention has occasionally been applied in nonconstitutional cases. *Louisiana
Power & Light Co. v. Thibodaux*,[7] for example,
ordered a district court in a diversity case to
abstain from resolving an unclear issue of state
law in order to avoid the risk of state-federal
friction in the sensitive context of the power of
eminent domain. The ambiguity of state law in
*Thibodaux* was crucial, for on the same day the
Court refused abstention in another eminent-
domain case in which the meaning of state law
was plain.[8] Yet the Supreme Court has made
clear that the ambiguity of state law is not enough
to support abstention; there must be in addition
either an unusually strong state interest, as in
*Thibodaux*, or a substantial constitutional

---

[6]Examining Board v. Flores de Otero, 426 U.S. 572 (1976).
[7]360 U.S. 25 (1959).
[8]Allegheny County v. Mashuda Co., 360 U.S. 185.

question that may be avoided by state decision of the state-law question.[9]

## B. CERTIFICATION

Some of the difficulties of *Pullman* abstention are avoided by the practice, pioneered in Florida, of certifying state-law questions directly to the state Supreme Court. Some time is saved since the parties need not go through the lower state courts and since only a narrow question of law is presented. The Supreme Court has endorsed certification as well as abstention.[10] No federal statute, however, authorizes the practice; the question of its legitimacy remains.

In contrast to the rule in abstention cases, several courts of appeals regularly certify questions to state courts on the basis of unclear state law alone. The Supreme Court, while reaffirming that "the mere difficulty in ascertaining local law is no excuse for remitting the parties to a state tribunal for the start of another lawsuit," appears to have endorsed certification under just such circumstances – although in the case before it the argument for certification was strengthened by the fact that the law in question was not that of the state in which the district court sat.[11]

---

[9]Meredith v. Winter Haven, 320 U.S. 228 (1943).
[10]Clay v. Sun Ins. Office, 363 U.S. 207 (1960).
[11]Lehman Bros. v. Schein, 416 U.S. 386 (1974).

## C. *BURFORD* AND *ALABAMA*

Occasional Supreme Court decisions have gone beyond *Pullman* by ordering not abstention but outright dismissal of suits challenging determinations made by state administrative agencies that do not fall within the limited strictures of § 1342, even in the absence of any suggestion that state law itself was unclear. In the best known of these decisions, *Burford v. Sun Oil Co.,*[12] the Court declined to review an order granting a permit to drill for oil, invoking "the nonlegal complexity" of the state's oil-conservation scheme, the "great public importance" of the subject, and the state's policy of promoting uniformity of decision by centralizing review in a single court. In *Alabama Public Service Comm. v. Southern Ry*[13], in contrast, the Court ordered dismissal of a suit challenging the refusal to permit abandonment of a short interstate rail route because the constitutional question was "local" and because Alabama, like Texas in *Burford*, had attempted to centralize judicial review.

It is worth repeating that decisions of this nature are comparatively rare. It has never occurred to the Court, for example, to forbid federal courts to examine state administrative orders in

---

[12]319 U.S. 315 (1943).

[13]341 U.S. 341 (1951).

ordinary welfare or school-segregation cases. In *Quackenbush v. Allstate Ins. Co*,[14] moreover, the Court held that a suit for damages could *never* be dismissed on *Burford* grounds. In most cases "federal courts ha[d] a strict duty to exercise the jurisdiction . . . conferred upon them by Congress"; in ordinary actions at law abstention had been allowed only to "postpone[] adjudication," not to deny it; dismissal was permissible only when the court had "discretion to grant or deny relief," namely in suits seeking equitable or declaratory remedies.

It was not easy for the Court to reconcile this conclusion with its 1981 decision in *Fair Assessment in Real Estate Ass'n v. McNary*,[15] which without statutory backing extended the ban on enjoining the collection of state taxes to actions for damages; but at least *Quackenbush* was a significant step in the right direction.

## D. EXHAUSTION OF ADMINISTRATIVE REMEDIES

It is familiar law that a federal court will ordinarily refuse to review the action of a federal administrative agency until the petitioner has exhausted her administrative remedies. Exhaustion serves to avoid piecemeal interruption

---

[14]517 U.S. 706(1996).
[15]454 U.S. 100.

of administrative processes, to eliminate unnecessary judicial effort, and to secure the views of
agency experts on questions within their compe-
tence. Its legal support lies in negative implication from the common statutory provisions for
review of "final" federal administrative
action;[16] in such equitable principles as public
consequences, adequate legal remedies, and the
lack of irreparable harm; and (in extreme
cases) in the constitutional requirement of a ripe
controversy.

At one time the Supreme Court said that considerations of federalism gave the exhaustion
doctrine "especial force" when a state rather than
a federal order was challenged.[17] In 1982,
however, in *Patsy v. Board of Regents*,[18] the Court
held that a federal court could not require a
litigant to exhaust state administrative remedies
in an action brought under § 1983, emphasizing
that statute's purpose – shared, of course, by all
federal jurisdictional provisions – "to interpose
the federal courts between the States and the
people." The Court was unfazed by precedents
allowing abstention and even dismissal in §
1983 cases, including the *McNary* case
respecting state taxes. The distinction seems
backwards, for dismissal deprives a plaintiff of
his right to a federal forum entirely, while
exhaustion produces only delay; once state

---

[16]Darby v. Cisneros, 509 U.S. 137 (1993).
[17]Natural Gas Pipeline Co. v. Slattery, 302 U.S. 300 (1937).
[18]457 U.S. 496.

administrators have had their say, the litigants are free to return to federal court.

## E. DOMESTIC RELATIONS, PROBATE, AND PENDING ACTIONS

Somewhat related to abstention is the established principle that, despite the presence of diversity, federal courts have no jurisdiction to grant a divorce, to award alimony, to determine child custody, to probate a will, or to administer an estate.[19] The justification is nominally historical, as domestic and probate matters are said to have been neither "legal" nor "equitable" in English practice, as predecessors of the present statutes required, but ecclesiastical. As Judge Posner has demonstrated, this reasoning is unpersuasive; there were no ecclesiastical courts in the United States in 1789. A more convincing explanation is that, as in *Burford* and *Alabama*, the grant of federal jurisdiction is interpreted to avoid interfering with "a state policy of channeling" litigation to specialized courts.[20]

This rationale neatly explains the limits of the domestic-relations and probate doctrines. The Supreme Court in *Markham v. Allen*,[21] for

---

[19]See, e.g., Barber v. Barber, 62 U.S. 582 (1859); Markham v. Allen, 326 U.S. 490 (1946).

[20]Hamilton v. Nielsen, 678 F.2d 709, 710 (7th Cir. 1982).

[21]See note 18 supra.

example, permitted a federal action to establish a claim against a decedent's estate on the ground that such a complaint was historically cogniz- able outside the probate court and left "undisturbed the orderly administration of dece- dent's estate." Similarly, the Seventh Circuit in 1982 allowed a federal action for compensatory damages for abduction of a child in violation of a state custody decree, emphasizing that in the state whose decree was in issue the tort suit "would be litigated as an independent civil ac- tion and not as an appendix to the custody pro- ceeding."[22]

In 1877 the Supreme Court held that the pendency of related litigation in a state court did not require a federal court to dismiss an action within its jurisdiction.[23] Later decisions, how- ever, have sometimes allowed lower courts to stay their hands pending related state-court proceedings, in recognition of the inefficiency of duplicative litigation. The most significant Supreme Court decisions to this effect are *Brill- hart v. Excess Ins. Co.*,[24] which relied on the "discretionary" nature of declaratory relief and stressed that the action was based on state law, and *Colorado River Water Conservation Dist. v. United States*,[25] which relied essentially on the desirability of avoiding "piecemeal litigation"

---

[22]Lloyd v. Loeffler, 694 F.2d 489.
[23]Stanton v. Embrey, 93 U.S. 548.
[24]316 U.S. 491 (1942).
[25]424 U.S. 800 (1976).

of matters that might adequately be resolved in the context of a "comprehensive" state system for adjudication of water rights. *Colorado* seems to take a narrower view of the proper occasion for such a stay than had several lower courts, branding such occasions as "exceptional" in light of the "virtually unflagging obligation of the federal courts to exercise the jurisdiction given them."

## F. INJUNCTIONS AGAINST SUIT

### 1. Section 2283

Federal injunctions against state-court proceedings have long been thought to present special dangers of federal-state friction; and in 1793 Congress flatly enjoined that no [federal] "writ of injunction be granted to stay proceedings in any court of a state."

Unfortunately for simplicity, the Court found a number of exceptions to this apparently absolute language, most of them based on subsequent statutes that expressly or impliedly authorized injunctions against state court proceedings. In 1948, in the general revision of the Judicial Code, Congress returned to the problem and attempted to make clear exactly when an injunction would lie against state-court proceedings. Here is the current statute in its entirety:

> A court of the United States may not grant an injunction to stay proceedings in a State court except as expressly authorized by Act of Congress, or where necessary in aid of its jurisdiction, or to protect or effectuate its judgments.

Unfortunately this language has not fully achieved the revisers' expectations.

### a. "Expressly Authorized"

The first exception allows an injunction against state-court proceedings when "expressly authorized by Act of Congress." The Interpleader Act, for example, says in so many words that the federal court may "enter its order restraining . . . [the claimants] from instituting or prosecuting any proceeding in any State or United States court" respecting the subject of a federal interpleader action (28 U.S.C. § 2361).

Before 1948, however, several exceptions had been based on statutes that were considerably less explicit, and the revisers said their intention was "to cover all [preexisting] exceptions." The Bankruptcy Act, for example, says only that other proceedings "shall be stayed," the law providing for limitation of shipowners' liability only that other proceedings "shall cease." It was reasonable enough for the Court to conclude that injunctions against state proceedings were necessarily implied to carry out such requirements,

but the authorization is scarcely "express." Yet
the revisers clearly intended to permit injunctions in these cases under the "expressly authorized" provision.

In *Mitchum v. Foster*[26] the Supreme Court took
a giant step further in holding that 42 U.S.C. §
1983, which provides that only persons acting
under color of state law shall be "liable . . . in an
action at law, suit in equity, or other proper
proceeding" for deprivation of constitutional
rights, "expressly authorized" an injunction
against state court proceedings. "In order to
qualify as an exception," the Court said (I kid
you not!), "[a] federal law need not expressly authorize an injunction of a state court proceeding." All that was required was that the statute
create "a specific and uniquely federal right or
remedy, enforceable in a federal court of equity,
that could be frustrated if the federal court were
not empowered to enjoin a state court proceeding." Having thus read out of § 2283 the central
requirement that the authorization be "express,"
the Court proceeded to find that the inadequacy of
state-court remedies had been the reason for
enactment of § 1983 – which could be said as well
of every grant of federal jurisdiction.

In *Vendo Co. v. Lektro-Vend Corp.*[27] the Court
was asked to hold, in light of *Mitchum*, that an

---

[26]407 U.S. 225 (1972).
[27]433 U.S. 623 (1977).

injunction against state proceedings was
"expressly authorized" by the Clayton Act, 15
U.S.C. § 26, which provides that "any person . . .
shall be entitled to sue for and have injunctive
relief, in any court of the United States . . . ,
against threatened loss or damage by violation
of the antitrust laws . . . when and under the
same conditions and principles as injunctive relief against threatened conduct that will cause
loss or damage is granted by courts of equity."
On the facts of the case the Court held the injunction unavailable. But there were four dissents, and two Justices in the majority voted to
deny relief only because there was no showing
that the party sought to be enjoined "was using the
state-court proceeding [itself] as an anticom-
petitive device."

b. "Necessary . . . in Aid of . . . Jurisdiction"

The revisers made clear that the exception for
injunctions "necessary . . . in aid of [federal]
jurisdiction" was intended to preserve decisions
permitting federal courts to which actions had
been removed to restrain further proceedings in
state court. The language suggests that it like-
wise preserves the preexisting exception permitting injunctions against state proceedings
"seeking to interfere with property in the custody

of the [federal] court" in actions in rem,[28] because
if the state court obtains the res the federal court
loses jurisdiction.

But an injunction will not lie to prevent multiple litigation of the same *in personam* claim in
state and federal courts, although if the state
court first entered judgment res judicata would
effectively prevent the exercise of federal jurisdiction.[29] Perhaps the best explanation for this
conclusion is that, while the state proceeding
may seriously impair the federal court's authority, there is no right to be free from suit in a state
court that Congress has allowed to exercise
concurrent jurisdiction.

The Court found a further limitation on the
"aid of . . . jurisdiction" provision in *Amalga-
mated Clothing Workers v. Richman Bros. Co.*[30]
In an earlier decision[31] the Court had allowed an
injunction against a state-court suit to enjoin
activities over which the National Labor Rela-
tions Board had exclusive jurisdiction. In *Richman*, however, the Court denied similar relief
although federal intervention was equally
"necessary" to prevent irreparable harm. In the
earlier case the injunction against state proceed-

---

[28]See Hyde Constr. Co. v. Koehring, 388 F.2d 501 (10th Cir.
1968).

[29]Atlantic Coast Line R.R. v. Brotherhood of Locomotive
Engineers, 398 U.S. 281 (1970).

[30]348 U.S. 511 (1955).

[31]Capital Service v. NLRB, 347 U.S. 501 (1954).

ings had been ancillary to a suit by the NLRB to enjoin the union's activity itself; in *Richman* it was the sole relief sought and thus not "in aid of" preexisting federal jurisdiction.

### c. "To Protect or Effectuate its Judgments"

The third exception in § 2283 permits a federal court to enjoin state-court proceedings in order "to protect or effectuate its judgments." This exception was included in order to overturn the Supreme Court's decision in *Toucey v. New York Life Ins. Co.*,[32] which had refused an injunction against relitigation of issues settled by a federal judgment although the losing party had filed five suits in different state courts on the same controversy. While res judicata was a defense to each of those state court proceedings, the burden of repeatedly making that defense was substantial.

### d. Implicit Exceptions and Proposals for Reform

The Court has repeatedly declared that § 2283 is subject to no implicit exceptions: "Legislative policy is here expressed in a clear-cut prohibition qualified only by specifically defined exceptions."[33] But the Court has not adhered to its

---

[32]314 U.S. 118 (1941).
[33]*Richman*, supra note 29.

own strict view. In *Leiter Minerals, Inc. v. United States*[34] it held § 2283 inapplicable to suits brought by the United States, invoking the maxim that "statutes which in general terms divest pre-existing rights or privileges will not be applied to the sovereign without express words to that effect." The Fourth Circuit took a cue from this decision in *Baines v. Danville*,[35] holding with more regard for policy than for the text that § 2283 allowed a temporary order preserving the status quo while the court determined whether the statute forbade a permanent injunction.

Finding the existing statute inadequate, the American Law Institute proposed some years ago to replace its three exceptions with seven of its own, which would have raised comparable interpretive problems. Perhaps the lesson to be drawn from this history is that courts will exercise judgment despite the most careful legislative efforts to circumscribe it, and that it would be the better part of valor to provide simply that federal courts may not enjoin state-court proceedings unless there is no other effective means of avoiding grave and irreparable harm.

---

[34]352 U.S. 220 (1957).
[35]337 F.2d 579.

## 2. Nonstatutory Limitations

Not only does § 2283 contain three explicit exceptions and one or two implicit ones to the policy against enjoining state-court proceedings. Although it does not explicitly say so, it applies only to proceedings that have already been instituted.[36] Nevertheless the issuance of injunctions not forbidden by § 2283 is far from automatic, for nonstatutory abstention doctrines have severely limited injunctions against state proceedings quite independently of the statute.

The leading case is *Younger v. Harris*,[37] decided in 1971. Assuming (as later held in *Mitchum*, supra) that § 1983 "expressly authorized" injunctions against state proceedings within the meaning of § 2283, the Court there refused such an injunction on the basis of the traditional equitable principle disfavoring injunctions against criminal proceedings, reinforced by considerations of what Justice Black referred to as "Our Federalism." Pending state criminal proceedings, the Court ruled, should be enjoined only if "the danger of irreparable loss is both great and immediate," and only if "the threat to the plaintiff's federal protected rights . . . cannot be eliminated by his defense against a single criminal prosecution."

---

[36]Dombrowski v. Pfister, 380 U.S. 479 (1965).
[37]401 U.S. 37.

The "cost, anxiety, and inconvenience of having to defend" against such a prosecution, the Court concluded in *Younger*, did not suffice. Neither, despite an apparent holding to the contrary in *Dombrowski v. Pfister*,[38] was the fact that the state law was challenged on the ground that its overbreadth "chilled" freedom of expression, since a federal injunction would not eliminate the chilling effect. On the other hand, when as in *Dombrowski* the state prosecution is brought in bad faith, ultimate vindication of the right not to be convicted is inadequate protection for the right not to be prosecuted at all, and the proceeding may be enjoined. Similarly, an injunction lies when the state tribunal that will hear the case is shown to be biased;[39] and unconstitutional pretrial incarceration may be enjoined because the injunction does not interfere with the prosecution and a defense at trial would not remedy the past wrong.[40] The test, as in pretrial habeas corpus (see chapter 9), turns on the adequacy of a state-court defense and the degree of interference with state-court proceedings.

The *Younger* principle has been extended to declaratory judgments, which the Court found to have substantially the same effect as injunctions;[41] to injunctions collateral to the merits of

---

[38]See note 35 supra.
[39]Gibson v. Berryhill, 411 U.S. 564 (1973).
[40]Gerstein v. Pugh, 420 U.S. 103 (1975).
[41]Samuels v. Mackell, 401 U.S. 66 (1971).

the prosecution, such as an order excluding illegally obtained evidence;[42] and to civil proceedings to abate a nuisance, because they served "to enforce . . . criminal laws." *Huffman v. Pursue, Ltd* (1975).[43]

The application of *Younger* to a civil case was a major extension. As the dissenters in *Huffman* pointed out, a criminal defendant can often return to federal court by seeking habeas corpus to review his conviction. In civil cases, on the other hand, a state-court judgment is conclusive; to deny an injunction is to deprive the litigant entirely of his federal forum. So far the Supreme Court has applied the doctrine in civil matters only when the state is a party[44] or when, as in proceedings involving contempt or the execution of judgments, "the administration of a State's judicial system" was involved.[45]

*Younger* itself was a § 1983 case; its conclusion that a criminal defendant had an adequate opportunity to protect his federal rights in state court seems difficult to square with the premise of § 1983, as emphasized both in *Patsy* and in *Mitchum*, that state courts are inadequate forums for the vindication of federal rights.

---

[42]Perez v. Ledesma, 401 U.S. 82 (1971).

[43]420 U.S. 592.

[44]See also Trainor v. Hernandez, 431 U.S. 434 (1977).

[45]Juidice v. Vail, 430 U.S. 327 (1977); Pennzoil Co. v. Texaco, Inc., 481 U.S. 1 (1987).

The policy bases of the *Younger* rule, in any event, help to define its limitations. In *Steffel v. Thompson*[46] the plaintiff, who had been threatened with arrest for trespass if he continued distributing handbills at a shopping center, sought a declaratory judgment that the state trespass statute was unconstitutional. The Court held that *Younger* was no bar. Because no prosecution had yet been commenced, there was no danger of duplicating or disrupting state-court proceedings. For the same reason, defense against state prosecution was a wholly inadequate remedy: "[A] refusal on the part of the federal courts to intervene . . . may place the hapless plaintiff between the Scylla of intentionally flouting state law and the Charybdis of foregoing what he believes to be constitutionally protected activity."

In *Doran v. Salem Inn*[47] the Supreme Court added that, while normally a declaratory judgment removed the necessity for enjoining a threatened prosecution, the *Steffel* principle permitted *preliminary* injunctions in such situations because there was no declaratory alternative. But the crux of the question, as defined in *Younger*, is whether leaving the federal plaintiff to defend a state prosecution would subject him to the risk of serious and irreparable harm, not simply whether a state prosecution is

---

[46]415 U.S. 452 (1974).
[47]421 U.S. 927 (1975).

pending when federal suit is filed. Thus when
there has been an agreement not to prosecute for
future violations until the results of a
contemplated test prosecution are known,[48] or
when a state prosecution is filed "before any
proceedings of substance on the merits" of a prior
federal complaint,[49] the Court has found no need
for federal intervention. One might think,
especially in light of the grant of preliminary
relief in *Doran*, that even a pending state
prosecution afforded inadequate protection to a
federal plaintiff seeking assurance that similar
conduct he wished to continue in the future was
protected. The Court held the contrary, however,
in *Roe v. Wade*.[50]

*Younger* has been applied with at least equal
force in refusing injunctive interference with
pending courts-martial, where the issue becomes
entwined with the exhaustion of administrative
remedies.[51] A Tenth Circuit decision requiring a
plaintiff to "exhaust administrative remedies"
by violating a military order to provoke a court-
martial[52] was later disavowed by the same court[53]
and cannot stand for reasons given by the
Supreme Court in *Steffel*.

---

[48]Beal v. Missouri Pac. R.R., 312 U.S. 45 (1941).

[49]Hicks v. Miranda, 419 U.S. 1018 (1975).

[50]410 U.S. 113 (1973).

[51]Schlesinger v. Councilman, 420 U.S. 738 (1975).

[52]Noyd v. McNamara, 378 F.2d 538 (1967).

[53]Miller v. United States Army, 458 F.2d 388 (1972).

## 3. State Injunctions Against Federal Proceedings

In *Donovan v. Dallas*[54] a litigant sought to raise in federal court an issue already settled by a state-court judgment. The state court enjoined him from doing so, and the Supreme Court reversed: State courts may enjoin proceedings in federal only to protect their jurisdiction in rem.

The Court gave reasons for this conclusion. First, while Congress had relaxed the once absolute ban on federal injunctions against state proceedings, it had never relaxed the converse prohibition. But Congress had never forbidden state injunctions against federal proceedings; its failure to amend a rule it had not enacted should not have been held to preclude the Court from reconsidering its own rule. Second, a state injunction denied the litigant the right given by the diversity statute to litigate in federal court. That this right is less than absolute is not a decisive answer, for one could agree that federal courts may refuse to exercise jurisdiction (forum non conveniens, abstention, etc.) without admitting that they may be ousted involuntarily by state action. But the Court's argument wholly fails to account for the acknowledged exception permitting injunctions to preserve in rem jurisdiction. Precedent, however, would have been

---

[54]377 U.S. 408 (1964).

justification enough for *Donovan*; if Congress
wishes to alter the longstanding interpretation of
the jurisdictional statute, it is free to amend.

# IX. APPELLATE AND COLLATERAL REVIEW

## A. SUPREME COURT REVIEW OF STATE JUDGMENTS

### 1. Federal and State Questions

Section 25 of the Judiciary Act of 1789 provided for Supreme Court review of state-court decisions, but only when a claim of federal right had been denied in the court below. This of course was the situation in which a state court could have the greatest adverse effect on federal policy. In 1914 the statute was extended to cases in which a state court had upheld a federal right, but in such cases review was to be by certiorari and therefore discretionary. The present statute, 28 U.S.C. § 1257, authorizes the Supreme Court to review state-court judgments in all cases involving rights under the federal Constitution, treaties, or statutes, but apparently not of cases arising under the federal common law, which still exists in some areas despite *Erie R.R. v. Tompkins.*

The Supreme Court upheld § 25 in 1816 in the famous case of *Martin v. Hunter's Lessee.*[1] The state of Virginia had attempted to confiscate land owned by a British subject; on an earlier appeal the Court had held that this action offended a

---

[1] 14 U.S. 304.

treaty. The state court refused to obey the mandate, arguing that the Supreme Court could not constitutionally review a state-court decision. The Supreme Court reversed again, relying in part upon the constitutional text: Article III extended the judicial power to "all" cases arising under the Constitution, and some such cases were brought in state courts.

As the judge below had observed, this argument proved too much: It would equally justify review of British, Canadian, or French courts in any case in which they applied a law of the United States. More persuasively, the Court added that Supreme Court review of state courts was necessary to achieve the purposes of the constitutional provision, namely to protect federal rights and ensure the uniformity of federal laws.

Generally speaking, as held in *Murdock v. Memphis*[2] in 1875, the Supreme Court's power to review state-court judgments extends only to federal questions. Supreme Court review of decisions respecting state law, the Court reasoned, was not necessary either to vindicate federal rights or to promote uniformity, and it would significantly impair the states' power to define their own laws. Thus there is no supplemental jurisdiction over state claims when the Supreme Court reviews a state-court judgment, and no

---

[2]87 U.S. 590

need for it either. To turn away the state claim in such a case does not result in multiple litigation; the claim has already been determined.

## 2. Adequate State Grounds

Thus, in general, the Supreme Court can review federal but not state questions decided by state courts. *Jankovich v. Indiana Toll Road Comm.*[3] illustrates an important limitation on this jurisdiction: The Court cannot review even the federal issue if the judgment is supported by an adequate and independent state ground.

The state court in *Jankovich* had held that a local ordinance violated *both* the federal and state constitutions. Under *Murdock* the Supreme Court had no jurisdiction to review the state question. A Supreme Court determination that the ordinance did not offend the federal Constitution, therefore, would not have affected the result; the ordinance would still have been invalid under the state constitution. Thus the case was moot; to decide the federal question would have been to render an advisory opinion.

Some caution is in order in administering this principle. It is not true that the Supreme Court can never review a judgment based on both federal and state grounds. For when a state court

---

[3]379 U.S. 487 (1965).

concludes that its law violates *neither* the federal nor the state constitution, a decision that the law does violate the federal Constitution will indeed require a reversal. In such a case the state ground is not adequate to sustain the judgment, and the Supreme Court may review the federal question. Whether the Court has jurisdiction, in other words, depends upon whether its decision of the federal question may affect the result reached by the court below.

Even when the state-law ground is broad enough to sustain the judgment, the Supreme Court may review the federal question if the state ground is not independent of the federal. In *Delaware v. Prouse*,[4] for example, the state court concluded that a search offended the Fourth Amendment and that, because the state constitution was "substantially similar" to the federal, it "necessarily" offended the state constitution as well. Reasoning that if it disagreed as to the meaning of federal law the state court might change its interpretation of the state constitution, the Supreme Court took jurisdiction: Its decision might well alter the outcome of the case.

A third limitation on the adequate state ground doctrine was established in *Martin v. Hunter's Lessee* itself. The treaty with Britain forbade only future confiscations, not those that

---

[4] 440 U.S. 648 (1979).

had already occurred. The state court held that the land in question had been escheated before the treaty was approved. The Supreme Court reversed, holding that the state court had misconstrued its own law and that the land had not been escheated until after the treaty. When a threshold issue of state law must be resolved in order to reach the federal question, this limited review of state questions is essential to prevent states from defeating federal rights by distorting their own law.

There are many similar cases. In *Indiana ex rel. Anderson v. Brand*,[5] for example, a public-school teacher alleged that the state had impaired the obligation of her contract by repealing a statute that guaranteed her tenure. The state court denied relief on the ground that there was no contract to impair, but the Supreme Court reversed. Whether there had been a contract was a question of state law, but the state court had got it wrong: There was a contract, and it had been impaired.

Similarly, in *Ward v. Love County*[6] a state court refused relief to Indians claiming a federal immunity from state taxation on the ground that they had paid the tax voluntarily. The Supreme Court held there was no evidence to support this finding. In short, a state court is not

---

[5]303 U.S. 95 (1938).
[6]253 U.S. 17 (1920).

permitted to twist either its own law or the facts relevant to its application in order to cheat a litigant out of a federal right.

But the *Ward* case suggests a fourth limitation on the adequate-state-ground doctrine. Even if the state law had expressly denied a remedy to persons in the plaintiffs' position, the result would have been the same. For an unconstitutional state ground is not an adequate one; and a rule precluding suit to recover taxes illegally collected would deprive the taxpayer of property without due process of law.

*Henry v. Mississippi,*[7] decided in 1965, illustrates the application of the adequate state ground doctrine in a procedural context. The state court admitted that illegally obtained evidence had been introduced in a criminal trial. It refused to reverse the conviction, however, because the defendant had failed to object at the time it was introduced. The question for the Supreme Court was whether this state-law ground was adequate to support the judgment.

Application of the adequate state ground doctrine, Justice Brennan argued, was different when the state law was procedural:

Where the ground involved is substantive, the determination of the federal question cannot

---

[7]379 U.S. 443.

affect the disposition if the state court decision on the state law question is allowed to stand. . . . A procedural default which is held to bar challenge to a conviction in state courts . . . prevents implementation of the federal right. . . . When and how defaults in compliance with state procedural rules can preclude our consideration of a federal question is itself a federal question.

Justice Brennan's conclusion is unassailable, but his distinctions do not hold water. In *Henry* itself, where the state ground was procedural, the Court could reverse the judgment only by displacing the state court's conclusion that the defendant had forfeited his remedy; and such cases as *Martin*, *Brand*, and *Ward* demonstrate that substantive as well as procedural grounds may prevent implementation of federal rights.

The real question in *Henry* was whether, as in *Ward*, the state ground was unconstitutional because it effectively denied a federal right.

The Supreme Court might plausibly have held that the procedure for raising federal rights in state courts was governed entirely by federal law. In the converse situation, federal courts in diversity suits based on state substantive law must apply state procedural rules having a significant effect on state policy.[8] However, just as a state court enforcing the law of another state is generally permitted to follow its own procedures,

---

[8]See the discussion in chapter 6.

the Supreme Court ordinarily allows state law to govern the raising of federal issues in state courts in order to effectuate the state's interest in an orderly judicial system.

Justice Brennan cut to the essence of the problem in *Henry*: A state procedural ground would be permitted to preclude consideration of a federal claim only if its application serves a legitimate state interest. Otherwise, he implied, application of the state rule would offend the Supremacy Clause because it unreasonably interfered with the enforcement of federal law.

Brennan's application of this exemplary principle to the case before him, however, left something to be desired. Application of the Mississippi rule requiring an immediate objection to the introduction of evidence, he suggested, served no purpose in *Henry* because the defendant's objection at the close of the state's case enabled the judge to redress the wrong by instructing the jury to disregard the evidence. It is hard to believe he really had such confidence in a jury's ability to ignore incriminating testimony whose reliability was not in question; prejudice to the defendant could have been safely avoided only by ordering a costly new trial.

The Court in *Henry* did not actually decide whether the state ground was adequate. It remanded the case for a determination whether the failure to object at the time the evidence was introduced had been deliberate. If a litigant chooses not to take advantage of the opportunity to raise an issue in the trial court, the Court seemed to be saying, he should not be permitted to raise it on appeal.

Finally, a state-court opinion may not always clearly reveal whether or not the judgment rests on an independent state ground. Before 1983 the Supreme Court had toyed with no fewer than four solutions to this problem. On occasion it would dismiss because the judgment *might* rest on a state ground. In at least one case it did the opposite, taking jurisdiction because the judgment *might not* rest on a state ground. More often, however, the Court sought to find out what the state court had actually done – either by holding the case while the parties sought a clarifying order or by vacating the decision below. In *Michigan v. Long*,[9] however, the Court resolved the confusion by announcing that henceforth it would run out to embrace any constitutional question that might be lurking around its door: "[W]hen the adequacy and independence of any possible state ground is not clear from the face of the opinion, we will accept as the most reasonable explanation that the state court decided the case the way it did because it believed that federal law required it to do so."

---

[9] 463 U.S. 1032 (1983).

## B. MISCELLANEOUS PROBLEMS

### 1. Appeal, Certiorari, and Certification

Originally the Supreme Court's entire jurisdiction was mandatory: The Court had to take the
case if it came within its jurisdiction. Because of
the increasing burden on the Court, Congress by
means of the discretionary writ of certiorari has
progressively reduced the area of mandatory
jurisdiction. As the result of a 1988 amendment
the Court's appellate jurisdiction is now almost
entirely discretionary; a petitioner for certiorari
must convince the Court that his case is
important enough that it ought to be heard. The
remaining exception is 28 U.S.C. § 1253, which
provides for mandatory appeal from district
courts composed of three judges, principally in
actions to enjoin legislative apportionments on
constitutional grounds.

In addition to the appeal and certiorari jurisdiction, § 1254 empowers the Supreme Court to
decide questions of law certified to it by the courts
of appeals. The statute looks permissive: The
Supreme Court "may" give answers to a certified
question. The commentators tend to say it *must*
do so, but the Court has developed rules for
limiting its jurisdiction. In *Wisniewski v.
United States*,[10] for example, the Court held that a
court of appeals ought not to employ the certi-

---

[10]353 U.S. 901 (1957).

fication procedure to resolve a conflict among its own judges. In general, the Court added, it was the job of the court of appeals to decide its own cases, not to pass the buck upstairs. Certification was proper only in unusual situations, such as when the identical question was already pending before the Supreme Court or when, as in the case of Governor Ross Barnett's demand for a jury trial in a contempt case, the court of appeals itself was equally divided and there was no lower court opinion to affirm.

Since the power to certify questions was rarely used, Congress seriously considering abolishing it in 1948, when the Judicial Code was last extensively revised. Three Justices, including the usually fastidious Justice Frankfurter, came down to testify that certification was a good practice, and it remains on the books today.

## 2. The Final-Judgment Rule

Interlocutory appeals interrupt ongoing proceedings, burden appellate courts, and often delay the ultimate resolution of disputes; the statutes generally disfavor them. § 1291 provides for appeal from "final decisions" of the district courts; § 1257 authorizes the Supreme Court to review "final judgments" of state tribunals.

Thus, while the grant of a motion to dismiss for failure to state a claim terminates the case and is therefore appealable, the denial of such a motion contemplates further proceedings at the trial level, and there can normally be no appeal. Similarly, when a motion for a new trial is denied, the court will enter a final judgment, and an appeal may follow. When a new-trial motion is granted, proceedings in the trial court are not over; again, in most cases, there can be no immediate appeal.

On occasion, however, interlocutory appeal can save time or prevent irreparable harm, and Congress accordingly has made several exceptions to the final-decision rule. Section 1292(a), for example, provides for immediate review of many interlocutory federal orders respecting injunctions. In many cases, Congress reasoned, the grant or denial of an interlocutory injunction may effectively decide the merits, and irreparable harm can be avoided only by immediate review.

Section 1292(b) authorizes a federal district judge to certify for interlocutory appeal any "controlling" and debatable issue of law whose immediate decision "may materially advance the termination of the litigation," but the courts of appeals need not entertain the appeal. Rule 54(b) of the Federal Rules of Civil Procedure permits additional interlocutory appeals by allowing trial judges to enter judgment on part of a case before the rest of it is resolved.

A further avenue of interlocutory review is the All Writs Act, 28 U.S.C. §1651, which allows appellate courts to issue writs of mandamus or prohibition where "necessary or appropriate in aid of" their own jurisdiction. Rejecting the argument that this provision could be invoked only to prevent the appellate court from being ousted of jurisdiction e.g., by transfer of the case to another circuit), the Supreme Court in *La Buy v. Howes Leather Co.*[11] held the "in aid of jurisdiction" requirement satisfied in any case in which the appellate court could ultimately review a final judgment. Nevertheless, the Court has made clear that these writs may be used only in exceptional cases, in order not to undermine the general policy against piecemeal appeals. According to one thoughtful observer, mandamus or prohibition is most likely to lie when the challenged order "was made without jurisdiction, . . . , is characteristic of an erroneous practice likely to reoccur . . . , [or] exemplifies a novel and important question in need of guidelines for the future resolution of similar cases."

Section 1254 allows the Supreme Court to review court-of-appeals cases before judgment, across the board. This provision not only allows review of interlocutory court-of-appeals orders, but also allows the Court to bypass the court of appeals entirely by taking a case as soon as it is filed in the appellate court. According to

---

[11]352 U.S. 249 (1957).

Supreme Court Rule 11, this power will be exercised only in cases of immediate public importance. It was used in the steel seizure case[12] and in *United States v. Nixon*,[13] which involved the Watergate tapes. Yet the Court refused certiorari before judgment in the court of appeals in the Little Rock segregation case[14], which one might have thought presented comparable urgency, and it has granted immediate review, usually in order to consolidate cases presenting similar issues, in cases of no great urgency at all.

It is not always obvious whether a decision or judgment is "final" for purposes of appeal, and the Supreme Court has severely watered down the requirement in recent years as applied to both state and federal decisions.

In *Construction Laborers v. Curry*,[15] for example, a state trial court had denied a temporary injunction in a case involving a labor dispute. The state supreme court had reversed and sent the case back for further proceedings. Though the state-court proceedings were not over, the Supreme Court granted immediate review to determine whether the Taft-Hartley Act preempted the state court's jurisdiction.

---

[12]Youngstown Sheet & Tube Co. v. Sawyer, 343 U.S. 579 (1952).

[13]418 U.S. 683 (1974).

[14]Aaron v. Cooper, 357 F.2d 566 (8th Cir. 1958).

[15]371 U.S. 542 (1963).

There were two grounds for the decision. One was solid and longstanding: Since the merits of the case had been decided on the motion for temporary injunction, and since no other defenses were available, the entry of final judgment was a mere formality, and there was no reason to defer review.

The other ground was more difficult to square with the statutory requirement of a "final judgment." The issue of state-court jurisdiction, the Court said, was "collateral" to the merits, and immediate review was needed to prevent irreparable harm. Just such an argument led Congress in § 1292(a) to provide for interlocutory appeal of federal injunctive orders, but there is no such provision respecting state courts.

Acknowledging the two exceptions relied on in *Curry*, the Supreme Court in *Cox Broadcasting Corp. v. Cohn*[16] noted two others: The pendency of further state-court proceedings did not impair the finality of a judgment if those proceedings could not moot the federal question or if there would never be another opportunity to decide it.

These decisions and others led one commentator to conclude that a state-court judgment was "final" for purposes of Supreme Court review if the appeal raised an unsettled question that was likely to be dispositive of the case. The Court

---

[16]420 U.S. 469 (1975).

came close to embracing this formulation in *Cox*, where it entertained an appeal from a state-court decision that upheld the constitutionality of damages for publishing the name of a rape victim and remanded for trial, saying that to deny review would leave unsettled an important and decisive constitutional question and chill the exercise of First Amendment freedoms.

The foregoing cases dealt with the finality of state-court judgments under § 1257, but the Court has taken similar liberties with the finality requirement for review of federal decisions under § 1291. E.g., *Abney v. United States*[17] (holding "final" the denial of a motion to dismiss on double-jeopardy grounds); *Cohen v. Beneficial Indus. Loan Corp.*[18] (reviewing the applicability of a state law that required the plaintiff in a shareholder's action to post security for costs).

Yet in more recent years the Court has been reluctant to extend these precedents to other interlocutory rulings. *United States v. MacDonald*[19] refused to allow an appeal from the denial of a pretrial motion to dismiss for failure to afford a speedy trial, distinguishing *Abney* on the ground that the Double Jeopardy Clause gave a right not to be tried at all that could not be vindicated by later review. Similarly, *Coopers &*

---

[17] 431 U.S. 651 (1977).
[18] 337 U.S. 541 (1949).
[19] 435 U.S. 850 (1978).

*Lybrand v. Livesay*[20] rejected the so-called "death knell" doctrine, which had allowed immediate appeal from the refusal to certify a class action when the plaintiff's personal stake was so small that he could not be expected to continue the suit on an individual basis. The *Curry* principle of irreparable harm, which underlay both *Abney* and *Cohen* seemed applicable to *Coopers* as well; yet the Court significantly emphasized that a loose construction of the finality requirement would undermine the limitations Congress had placed on interlocutory review of federal decisions in § 1292(b).

Thus the Court seems to construe the finality requirement more strictly in reviewing federal than in reviewing state determinations. One might have expected the opposite, both because of federalism concerns and because of the difference in language: Justice Frankfurter once suggested that a final "decision" under § 1291 need not amount to a final "judgment" under § 1257. On the other hand, interlocutory appealability under § 1291 means interruption of an ongoing trial-court proceeding; under § 1257 the question is usually whether to review a state appellate decision after trial proceedings have already been appealed.

---

[20]437 U.S. 463 (1978).

## C. POST-CONVICTION REVIEW

### 1. The Issues Cognizable

In recent decades most state criminal convictions have been reviewed for constitutional error not by petition for certiorari in the Supreme Court under § 1257 but by petition for habeas corpus in the federal district courts. The law governing this "collateral" review of state-court judgments is quite complex and tends to change with every alteration in the membership of the Court.

The basic statutory provision regarding habeas corpus is 28 U.S.C. § 2241, which makes the writ available to any person who is "in custody in violation of the Constitution or laws or treaties of the United States." This does not now mean and never has meant that everyone whose conviction is tainted by an error of federal law is entitled to relief.

To begin with, until rather recently there were stringent limitations on the kinds of federal issues that could be raised on habeas corpus in attacking a criminal conviction. Habeas was initially essentially a device for testing the validity of *executive* detention; ordinary principles of finality precluded collateral attack on any judgment rendered by a competent court. Thus it used to be said that habeas could be employed to challenge a conviction only for lack of jurisdiction.

On at least two early occasions the Supreme Court allowed habeas review of questions that were not jurisdictional – double jeopardy and the constitutionality of the statute under which the petitioner had been convicted. But these decisions seem to have been considered exceptions to the general rule that habeas could not do service for an appeal.

Later cases, however, greatly extended the types of issues that could be raised on habeas corpus. In *Johnson v. Zerbst*,[21] while adhering to the formula that only jurisdictional questions could be raised, the Court concluded that denial of the right to counsel was such a fundamental error that it deprived a court of jurisdiction over the offense. In *Waley v. Johnston*[22] the Court abandoned the fiction of jurisdiction altogether, permitting a habeas petitioner to raise the question whether his guilty plea had been coerced because he could not effectively have raised it in the original proceeding.

In *Brown v. Allen*,[23] without mentioning the problem, the Court went still further, determining the voluntariness of a confession in a habeas case although the state court had already heard and decided the issue. As the Court made clear in *Fay v. Noia*[24] in 1963, every kind of federal

---

[21]304 U.S. 458(1938).
[22]316 U.S. 101 (1942).
[23]334 U.S. 443 (1953).
[24]372 U.S. 391.

constitutional question was now open to a state convict on habeas corpus, and *Kaufman v. United States*[25] seemed to say the same was true for a federal prisoner seeking an analogous remedy under 28 U.S.C. § 2255. Nevertheless, as will shortly appear, not every allegation of constitutional error will be considered on its merits in a habeas proceeding.

## 2. The Impact of a Prior State-Court Decision

*Brown v. Allen*, in which the state court had already rejected a coerced-confession claim, also raised the issue of res judicata: Even if the confession question fell within the jurisdiction of the federal habeas court, why wasn't the state-court determination of that question binding? 28 U.S.C. § 1738 would appear to make it so, for it requires federal courts to afford state judgments "the same full faith and credit . . . as they have . . . in the courts . . . from which they are taken."

Without referring to this statute, the Court in *Brown* held res judicata inapplicable in habeas cases. Justice Frankfurter attempted to tie this conclusion to the statutory grant of authority to issue the writ on behalf of a person "in custody in violation of the Constitution," but – as Justice Harlan would later explain – one who is held pursuant to a judgment that cannot be collater-

---

[25]394 U.S. 217 (1969).

ally attacked is not unconstitutionally in custody.

Nevertheless the Court's conclusion was correct. For § 2254(b), which was in force at the time of the *Brown* decision, precludes relief "unless . . . the applicant has exhausted the remedies available in the courts of the State." The clear implication is that federal relief may be available after state courts have passed upon the petitioner's claims; and thus § 2254(b) creates an exception to § 1738 and to the ordinary principles of res judicata.

It followed, said the Court in *Brown*, that questions of law and of ultimate fact – such as whether, if the defendant had been beaten by the police, his confession was involuntary – could be re-examined by a federal court de novo. On basic fact issues, however – such as whether the defendant had been beaten – a state-court finding should be respected absent a "vital flaw" in the state court's proceedings. This standard was modified in 1963 in *Townsend v. Sain*:[26] Even basic fact findings must be re-examined on habeas corpus unless the state court had afforded the defendant a "full and fair" hearing.

Recent amendments to the statute, however, have significantly reduced the scope of review of questions decided by state courts. Section 2254(d)

---

[26]372 U.S. 293.

now precludes reexamination of "any claim that was adjudicated on the merits in State court proceedings" unless the state court's adjudication

(1) resulted in a decision that was contrary to, or involved an unreasonable application of, clearly established Federal law, as determined by the Supreme Court of the United States; or

(2) resulted in a decision that was based on an unreasonable determination of the facts in light of the evidence presented in the State court proceedings.

It is clear that this provision limits redetermination of questions of law as well as fact, and § 2254(e) further limits the federal court's ability to take new evidence.

Moreover, since the decision of *Stone v. Powell*[27] in 1976, prior state-court consideration of at least one type of constitutional claim may preclude habeas corpus relief altogether. The petitioners in *Stone* argued that evidence used against them had been obtained by virtue of unconstitutional searches or seizures. In language reminiscent of *Townsend v. Sain*, the Court held this question could not be investigated on habeas because the state courts had afforded the prisoners "an opportunity for full and fair litigation" of their claims. In the case of evidence

---

[27]428 U.S. 465.

obtained by unlawful search or seizure, the Court noted, the exclusionary rule served not to improve the truth-finding process but to deter wrongdoing by the police; the marginal deterrence provided by affording a second opportunity to litigate the legality of the search did not justify the cost of reopening the proceeding.

The Court emphasized in *Stone* that it was neither holding the court without jurisdiction nor laying down principles to govern habeas litigation of "constitutional claims generally"; it was merely defining the scope of the exclusionary rule. Yet the Court has undertaken a similar balancing operation in holding *Stone* inapplicable to other specific issues. *Jackson v. Virginia*[28] held a full and fair state hearing did not preclude consideration of the question whether there was constitutionally adequate evidence to sustain a guilty verdict, because the issue was "central to the basic question of guilt or innocence." *Rose v. Mitchell*[29] similarly held *Stone* inapplicable to a claim of discrimination in grand-jury selection: There was greater need for a federal forum because the state courts were asked to review their own alleged violations, and less invasion of state interests because the defendant could be retried on the same evidence.

---

[28]443 U.S. 307 (1979).
[29]443 U.S. 545 (1979).

Just what constitutes "an opportunity for full and fair litigation" within the meaning of the *Stone* opinion remains unclear. The Supreme Court made no effort to define the term beyond the footnote reference "Cf. Townsend v. Sain." Although one of the *Townsend* criteria was whether the state finding was "fairly supported by the record," lower courts have understandably been reluctant to inquire under *Stone* into the correctness of a state-court search decision. Moreover, the Fifth Circuit has held, over dissent, that *Stone*'s reference to an "opportunity" for litigation means there need not always be an actual state hearing to preclude habeas corpus.[30] The defendant who fails to object in state court, the court said, has not been denied his opportunity; there is ample deterrence if the officer knows the state court will exclude improper evidence upon timely objection.

### 3. Procedural Defaults

The habeas applicant in the case just discussed lost his claim not because it had been previously decided, but because he had failed to raise it in the state court. Although res judicata often precludes litigation of issues that ought to have been tried before as well as those that were, res judicata, as we have seen, does not apply to habeas corpus. Moreover, while the *Stone*

---

[30]Caver v. Alabama, 577 F.2d 1188 (1978).

doctrine of an opportunity for full and fair litigation may be broad enough to cover search-and-seizure claims that ought to have been litigated in state court, the problem of procedural defaults in the original proceeding is not confined to search-and-seizure claims, and it has a separate history.

The prisoner in *Brown v. Allen*, as we know, had raised his constitutional objections in state court, and they had been decided against him. In the companion case of *Daniels v. Allen*[31] appeal papers had been filed one day too late, and the state court had refused to consider them. Holding habeas did not lie, the Court gave three reasons: Daniels had waived his federal rights by failing to appeal in time; he had failed to exhaust his state-court remedies as required by § 2254(b); and the judgment under which he was confined was supported by an adequate and independent state-law ground – the untimeliness of his appeal.

It may seem peculiar that greater preclusive effect was given to the failure to litigate an issue than to its actual decision; Brown was given a second review, while Daniels had no review at all. Yet the two decisions taken together had the advantage of equating the power of the district courts in habeas corpus with that of the Supreme Court on direct review, and thus of unloading on

---

[31]344 U.S. 443 (1953).

the district courts the increasing burden of reviewing state criminal convictions.

*Daniels* was repudiated in *Fay v. Noia*[32] in 1963. Waiver, the Court now said, did not mean forfeiture; it required the voluntary relinquishment of a known right. The exhaustion requirement, the Court added, applied only to remedies that were still available; it was not a forfeiture provision either. To forestall the argument that this construction would encourage litigants to frustrate the purpose of the exhaustion requirement by withholding their claims from state court, *Noia* declared that a prisoner who "deliberately bypassed" his state-court remedies would forfeit his federal remedy as well. The apparent source of this rule was § 2243, which directs the court to "dispose of the matter as law and justice require." The Court was later to say the same bypass standard applied on direct review in the Supreme Court, although in such a case there is no counterpart to § 2243.[33]

The most interesting aspect of *Noia*, however, was its holding that the adequate-state-ground doctrine did not apply to procedural questions on habeas corpus. The basis of that doctrine, the Court said, was that a judgment was immune from attack if supported by an adequate state

[32]372 U.S. 391.
[33]Henry v. Mississippi, supra.

ground; no judgment was necessary to support a habeas petition.

As Justice Harlan observed in dissent, however, a petitioner held pursuant to a state-court judgment is lawfully in custody until the judgment is set aside. Thus in a case like *Noia* the reasons underlying the adequate-state-ground doctrine were as applicable on habeas corpus as on direct review. To decide the federal question alone would run afoul of the prohibition on moot cases; to decide the state-law question would be beyond the Court's power under *Murdock v. Memphis*.

But to say the adequate-state-ground doctrine should have applied in *Noia* is not to say that the state ground in that case was adequate. As *Henry v. Mississippi* would soon make clear, the question was whether application of the state rule requiring a timely appeal imposed an unreasonable burden on the enforcement of a federal right. It would not have been implausible for the Court to find the state's procedural interest insufficient to justify the enormity of imprisonment on the basis of an unreliable confession.

In 1977, in *Wainwright v. Sykes*,[34] the Court abandoned the lenient approach toward procedural defaults it had displayed in *Noia*. Sykes sought habeas corpus on the ground that he had

---

[34]433 U.S. 72.

not been given adequate warnings under *Mi-randa v Arizona* before making incriminating statements. But he had not objected to the introduction of those statements at trial, as state law required, and the Court held this failure was fatal to his petition.

The Court invoked neither exhaustion nor waiver, nor did it bother to refute *Noia*'s argument against applying the adequate-state-ground doctrine. It did say that an adequate state ground would preclude review "in the federal courts," and it concluded that the state-law ground in the case before it would be adequate to bar direct Supreme Court review. But it stopped short of saying that habeas corpus too was barred by the adequacy of the state ground; instead it relied upon what it described as "the rule" laid down initially in *Davis v. United States*[35] in 1973.

Davis had been in federal rather than state prison, and the basis for holding that he could not object for the first time in a post-conviction motion to the makeup of his grand jury was that Rule 12(b)(2) of the Federal Rules of Criminal Procedure required such an objection to be made before trial. The next step was taken in *Francis v. Henderson*,[36] which applied the same "rule" to a state prisoner because "there is no reason to . . .

---

[35]411 U.S. 949.
[36]425 U.S. 536 (1976).

give greater preclusive effect to procedural defaults by federal defendants than to similar defaults by state defendants."

There was of course one very good reason for such a distinction: Federal Rule 12 was binding on the federal court, and the parallel state rule was not. *Francis* and *Sykes*, which extended its reasoning to the *Miranda* objection, seem to have created a judge-made doctrine of forfeiture in deference to state interests, without acknowledging that that was what they were doing. In both cases the Court added that the state rule would not bar habeas if, as under Rule 12(b), the prisoner made "a showing of cause for the noncompliance and . . . of actual prejudice resulting from the alleged constitutional violation."

The effect of these decisions is essentially to reinstate the adequate-state-ground doctrine in habeas-corpus proceedings attacking state criminal convictions. Later opinions have paraphrased them as holding that habeas is barred by an adequate state ground,[37] but the exception for "cause" and "prejudice" looks more flexible than past applications of the state-ground principle. Whether a state procedural rule that did not contain such an exception would now be held inadequate to bar *direct* review remains to be seen.

---

[37]E.g., Jackson v. Virginia, 443 U.S. 307 (1979).

On habeas corpus, at least, the crucial question has become what constitutes sufficient "cause" to excuse a procedural default. Simple attorney error does not qualify, although incompetence of counsel in the constitutional sense would.[38] Failure to raise a claim is excused if the claim is "so novel that its legal basis is not reasonably available to counsel,"[39] or if the state has concealed the evidence on which the claim is based.[40] Yet while the novelty of the claim may justify failure to raise it in the original proceeding, it may defeat habeas corpus on another ground; for under *Teague v. Lane*[41] most new constitutional limits on criminal procedure will not be retroactively applied on collateral review – lest a great many guilty convicts be entitled to a new trial after evidence of their guilt has disappeared.

## 4. Federal Prisoners

Habeas corpus lay for federal as well as state prisoners; indeed until 1867 it was available only to persons in federal custody. But habeas had to be sought in the district where the prisoner was confined, not where he had been convicted. In 1948 Congress enacted a new post-conviction remedy for federal prisoners in the district in

---

[38]Murray v. Carrier, 477 U.S. 478 (1986).
[39]Reed v. Ross, 468 U.S. 1 (1984).
[40]Amadeo v. Zant, 486 U.S. 214 (1988).
[41]109 U.S. 1060 (1989).

which they had been tried (28 U.S.C. § 2255). This remedy was meant to be as broad as habeas but to relieve the load on the courts in districts containing federal prisons and to entrust the task to a judge already familiar with the case.

The language of § 2255 is confusing and contradictory. The grounds for entertaining the motion seem narrower than those on which relief is to be granted, which cannot have been intended.

The operative language requires relief if the court finds "that the judgment was rendered without jurisdiction, or that the sentence imposed was not authorized by law or otherwise subject to collateral attack, or that there has been such a denial or infringement of the constitutional rights of the prisoner as to render the judgment vulnerable to collateral attack." The implication is that only a constitutional violation, and not every one, is enough to subject the "judgment," as opposed to the "sentence," to collateral attack. Yet the scope of the § 2255 remedy expanded along with habeas corpus for state prisoners during the 1960's. *Kaufman v. United States*, already mentioned, held that § 2255 embraced search-and-seizure claims, and a second case entitled *Davis v. United States*[42] held it applicable to the nonconstitutional claim that the regulation under which the prisoner had been convicted was invalid.

---

[42]419 U.S. 966 (1974).

This decision illustrates that the Court pays
less attention to the language of § 2255 than to its
purpose of providing a remedy as broad as
habeas; for habeas itself still lies whenever the §
2255 remedy is inadequate. But a dictum in
*Davis* and the later decision in *United States v.
Timmreck*[43] reaffirmed that § 2255 was available only to correct only those non-constitutional
defects that were "fundamental." That Davis
had arguably committed no crime was fundamental; that a defendant had been denied the
right to speak before being sentenced was not.[44]
The same standard applies to nonconstitutional
claims made by state prisoners on habeas corpus.[45]

The last important Supreme Court decision on
the effect of prior proceedings on a § 2255 motion
remains *Sanders v. United States*,[46] decided in
1963. As in habeas corpus for state prisoners, the
Court held res judicata inapplicable. But it
declared that a federal prisoner would be barred
from relitigating an issue that had been given
full and fair consideration on an earlier § 2255
motion. With regard to basic facts, *Townsend v.
Sain* then applied the same test to state prisoners.
But under *Sanders* even questions of law, which
for a state prisoner could then be determined de
novo, were not to be reexamined absent

---

[43]441 U.S. 780 (1979).
[44]Hill v. United States, 368 U.S. 424 (1962).
[45]Reed v Farley, 512 U.S. 339 (1994).
[46]375 U.S. 844.

"intervening change in the law" or other extraordinary circumstances

*Sanders* could have been rested on § 2255's provision that the court "shall not be required to entertain a second or successive motion for similar relief on behalf of the same prisoner." But it was not, and in *Kaufman* the Court suggested in dictum that the *Sanders* test might apply to the effect of an adjudication in the original proceeding too.

There were suggestions in both *Sanders* and *Kaufman* that the deliberate-bypass rule of *Fay v. Noia* might determine the effect of a procedural default upon a § 2255 application. In any event the first *Davis* case made clear that specific provisions of the Rules of Criminal Procedure might impose more stringent forfeiture requirements, and subsequent restrictions on habeas for state prisoners suggest that the Court will be less receptive to the claims of federal prisoners as well.

## 5. Military Prisoners

As if all this were not complicated enough, yet another body of law governs the availability of post-conviction relief for military prisoners.

At one time the Supreme Court was wont to say that military prisoners could get habeas corpus only to challenge the jurisdiction of the court-martial that convicted them. Most such statements, however, were made before *Johnson v. Zerbst*, when *nobody* could raise questions other than jurisdiction on habeas corpus. There was no suggestion that review was narrower in military than in other cases.

The leading Supreme Court case on military habeas corpus is still the 1953 decision in *Burns v. Wilson*,[47] in which there was no majority opinion. Only Justice Minton adhered to the old principle that only jurisdiction could be reviewed. Speaking for four Justices, Chief Justice Vinson stated the test in a form that lower courts have often repeated: The question is whether the military tribunal afforded a "full and fair hearing" on federal constitutional claims. A similar test had been applied to civil prisoners before *Brown v. Allen*, but five Justices made clear they thought habeas narrower for military than for civil prisoners.

Since *Burns v. Wilson* the Supreme Court has spoken only obliquely on military post-conviction review. *United States v. Augenblick*[48] (1969) was a suit for back pay in which a discharge based upon a court-martial was under attack. The first obstacle was 10 U.S.C. § 876, which makes military criminal proceedings "final and conclusive" and "binding" on the fed-

---

[47]346 U.S. 137.
[48]393 U.S. 348.

eral courts. This statute has been held not to bar habeas corpus because of the constitutional provision against suspension of the writ,[49] and the committee reports expressly recognized the habeas exception when the finality provision was recodified. The Court of Claims in *Augenblick* held § 876 did not bar back-pay suits either, but the Supreme Court held only that the issues raised – the necessity for corroboration and the right to examine witness statements – were not cognizable because not of constitutional dimension. Whether the same limitations would have applied to military habeas the Court did not say.

The Court added some useful dicta on military post-conviction review in *Schlesinger v. Councilman*,[50] which refused to allow an injunction against a pending court-martial because the plaintiff had failed to exhaust military remedies. The finality clause of § 876, the Court said, merely embodied normal principles of res judicata, which allowed not only habeas but other post-conviction remedies as well for "lack of jurisdiction or some other equally fundamental defect." But the Court added that "[g]rounds of impeachment cognizable in habeas proceedings may not be sufficient to warrant other forms of collateral relief," for whether the issue may be

---

[49]Gusik v. Schilder, 340 U.S. 128 (1950).
[50]420 U.S. 738 (1975).

raised may turn in part upon "the gravity of the harm from which relief is sought."

Given this lack of guidance from above, the lower courts divided as to the scope of post-conviction review of military tribunals. Several courts of appeals continued to say the test was that enunciated by the Chief Justice in *Burns v. Wilson*. Others, however, opened up a broader scope of military post-conviction review, as exemplified by *Calley v. Calloway*,[51] which laid down a four-point test: 1) The issue must be jurisdictional, constitutional, or "fundamental" in the sense of *Davis v. United States*. 2) On questions of "fact" the court will defer to military findings if there has been a "full and fair" hearing. 3) Questions of "law" will be resolved de novo. 4) Military findings that discipline requires different substantive rules will be given considerable deference on grounds of expertise.

With respect to the effect of procedural defaults in military proceedings on the availability of habeas corpus, the lower courts again are in disarray. Some have said if the issue was not raised the military did not afford a full and fair hearing, so the issue is reviewable. Others, anticipating the Fifth Circuit's response to *Stone v. Powell*, have said there was no denial of a full and fair hearing if the issue was not raised in time. The Fifth Circuit said *Fay v. Noia* applied

---

[51]519 F.2d 184 (5th Cir. 1975).

to military proceedings:[52] Absent a deliberate
bypass there was no forfeiture for failure to raise
the issue in time. Obviously this question must
be re-examined in light of *Wainwright v.
Sykes*.

Thus the scope of post-conviction review for
those convicted of military offenses remains
largely a mystery. In assessing what that scope
ought to be one should bear in mind, on the one
hand, that the military prisoner – like his state
counterpart and unlike the federal civil prisoner
– may never have had a prior opportunity to
present his federal arguments in an Article III
federal court. On the other hand, until recently a
broad scope of habeas for military convicts would
arguably have been inconsistent with the policy
of military independence that appeared to
underlie Congress's consistent refusal to provide
for direct civilian review of military
convictions. Congress's decision to permit
Supreme Court review of certain decisions of the
Court of Appeals for the Armed Forces (28 U.S.C.
§ 1259) puts this question in a different light.

### 6. Custody, Prematurity, and Venue

Habeas corpus is not available to everyone
who has been unconstitutionally convicted of
crime; under § 2241 the writ may be issued only

---

[52]Williams v. Heritage, 323 F.2d 731 (1963).

on behalf of a person in "custody." Thus a convict who has simply been fined is not entitled to habeas corpus. On the other hand, it is not necessary that the petitioner be in jail.

In *Jones v. Cunningham*[53] the Supreme Court held that a convict on parole was in sufficient "custody" to support habeas corpus. He was subject, the Court said, to significant restraints on his liberty which were not shared by the public generally. He was not allowed to leave town, to move from one home to another, or to drive a car, without the consent of his parole officer. As precedent the Court relied on cases holding that habeas lay to test the right of aliens to enter the country even though, as the Court put it in *Jones*, they were "free to go anywhere else in the world." Similarly, said the Court, habeas was the appropriate vehicle for testing an allegedly unlawful induction into the military services and for determining which parent was entitled to custody of a child.

All this was reasonable enough, but in *Hensley v. Municipal Court*[54] the Court watered the custody requirement down beyond recognition in holding that a petitioner was "in custody" while released on his own recognizance pending review of a jail sentence. The dissenters protested that the sole restraint on Hensley was

---

[53]371 U.S. 236 (1963).
[54]411 U.S. 345 (1973).

the duty to appear in court when called: He was "under no greater restriction than one who had been subpoenaed to testify." The Court was obviously concerned about the arbitrariness of an interpretation that would have required the petitioner to spend ten minutes in jail in order to obtain review.

It is also possible that one may be held in unconstitutional custody although one is not entitled to complete freedom. *In re Bonner*,[55] for example, held that habeas lay when the petitioner had been locked up in the wrong jail. The lower courts were slow to follow the implications of this decision with respect to unconstitutional prison conditions, but the Supreme Court gave such claims a boost by its almost parenthetical remark in *Wilwording v. Swenson*[56] that allegations of inadequate prison facilities and physical mistreatment were "cognizable on federal habeas corpus" as well as under the civil-rights statute, 42 U.S.C. § 1983.

Until rather recently the doctrine of prematurity had been a serious obstacle to a petitioner seeking to challenge one of two or more consecutive sentences by habeas corpus. A future sentence could not be challenged while a valid sentence was being served, because the petitioner was not unlawfully in custody. Lower courts had

---

[55]151 U.S. 242 (1894).
[56]404 U.S. 249 (1971).

held that the first sentence could not be attacked while it was being served either: Even if it were set aside, the prisoner would still be lawfully in custody under the unchallenged second sentence. The Supreme Court disapproved the latter position in *Walker v. Wainwright*[57] and the former in *Peyton v. Rowe*,[58] stretching the language of § 2241 in recognition of the desirability of reviewing convictions while the evidence was still available and before the prisoner began doing time he was arguably entitled not to serve.

Whether *Walker* and *Rowe* apply to federal prisoners seeking relief under § 2255 is not altogether clear, for in addition to requiring that the applicant be in federal custody that section limits the writ to persons "claiming the right to be released." The Fourth Circuit argued in dictum that the requirement would be satisfied in a case like *Rowe* because the petitioner sought release "from all of the burdens of the invalid sentence." A better argument might be, as the Supreme Court said in another context in *United States v. Hayman*,[59] that § 2255 was intended to be as broad as habeas. Moreover, the statute itself provides that if the remedy it provides is insufficient, habeas will lie.

---

[57]390 U.S. 335 (1968).
[58]391 U.S. 54 (1968).
[59]342 U.S. 205 (1952).

In *Carafas v. LaVallee*[60] the petitioner had been in custody when he filed for habeas corpus but had been released before his case was decided. The Supreme Court held him nonetheless entitled to habeas corpus. The custody requirement applied only at the time the case was filed; the case was not moot because it involved a felony conviction that had collateral consequences after the sentence expired.

In *Braden v. 30th Judicial Circuit Court*[61] the petitioner was in an Alabama prison but was attacking the proceedings of Kentucky officials respecting a Kentucky offense. Section 2241 authorizes federal judges to issue habeas "within their respective jurisdictions," and an earlier decision had construed the quoted words to require custody in the district where the writ was sought. Nevertheless, observing that Kentucky was a more appropriate place to try a case concerning a Kentucky offense, the Supreme Court upheld the power of the Kentucky district court to hear the petition: § 2241 required no more than that the court issuing the writ have jurisdiction over the custodian." Once again practical wisdom prevailed over the language of a poorly drafted statute.

### 7. Exhaustion of State Remedies

---

[60]391 U.S. 234 (1968).
[61]410 U.S. 484 (1973).

Notwithstanding the flat statutory command that habeas corpus lay on behalf of all persons "restrained of . . . liberty" in violation of federal law, the Supreme Court in *Ex parte Royall*[62] in 1886 refused to allow a federal court to issue a writ of habeas that would interfere with a pending state criminal proceeding. In order to avoid "unnecessary conflict" between state and federal courts, the Court decreed, a litigant must exhaust state-court remedies before seeking federal relief. This requirement was subsequently extended to petitions attacking convictions that had already been obtained, and Congress codified this aspect of the doctrine in 1948: No writ may be granted on petition of "a person in custody pursuant to the judgment of a State court" unless he has "exhausted the remedies available in the courts of the State." 28 U.S.C. § 2254(b).

The evident purpose of this provision was to afford state courts a final opportunity to re-examine the correctness of their own convictions, but literally the exhaustion requirement applies to every habeas petition filed by a state convict, whether or not he challenges his conviction. The Court wisely rejected this literal interpretation in *Wilwording v. Swenson*,[63] allowing a state prisoner to challenge the conditions of his confinement under 42 U.S.C. § 1983 without exhausting state remedies. However, concerned

---

[62]117 U.S. 241.
[63]404 U.S. 249 (1971).

lest litigants undermine the exhaustion requirement by employing § 1983 in "traditional" habeas corpus cases, a divided Supreme Court in *Preiser v. Rodriguez*[64] held state-court remedies must be exhausted before challenging the loss of good-time credits based on prison behavior because the question affected the "duration of the confinement itself." The line drawn by the Court conforms neither to the language nor to the purpose of the statutory requirement.

Even where it applies, the exhaustion requirement is not absolute. To begin with, a petitioner need not make repeated applications to the state courts based upon the same issue.[65] Moreover, the statute does not require exhaustion if state remedies are "ineffective" to protect the petitioner's rights. Thus a long line of Fifth Circuit decisions has held that exhaustion is not required if it is "futile," that is, if "the state's highest court has recently rendered an adverse decision in an identical case, and if there is no reason to believe that the state court will change its position."[66] On the other hand, the Second Circuit has held the mere fact that exhaustion would require a petitioner to spend the weekend in jail while waiting for the state appellate court

---

[64]411 U.S. 475 (1973).
[65]Brown v. Allen, 344 U.S. 443 (1953).
[66]E.g., Layton v. Carson, 479 F.2d 1275 (1973).

to meet insufficient to justify immediate federal intervention.[67]

When habeas is sought before conviction, the courts are likely to insist not only that the question be first decided by the state courts but also that the trial be completed, for habeas will be unnecessary if the petitioner is acquitted on some other ground. Once again, however, the exhaustion requirement is not absolute. In *Braden v. 30th Judicial Circuit Court*,[68] for example, the Supreme Court allowed federal habeas to determine the right of the petitioner to be brought speedily to trial. Noting that the state courts had already rejected this claim, the Court said Braden was seeking not to litigate "a federal defense to a criminal charge" but to "demand enforcement of the . . . obligation to bring him promptly to trial" and concluded that his petition would not "forestall a state prosecution" but merely require the state to "provide him with a state court forum." Similarly, in *Fain v. Duff*[69] the Fifth Circuit entertained a pre-trial habeas petition based upon double jeopardy after an unsuccessful state-court appeal: To set a sentence aside after conviction would be inadequate, since the Constitution protected the petitioner not only from a second punishment but

---

[67]United States ex rel. Goodman v. Kehl, 456 F.2d 863 (1972).
[68]410 U.S. 484 (1973).
[69]488 F.2d 218 (1973).

also from the "rigors and dangers" of the second trial.

## 8. Other Post-Conviction Remedies

Criminal Rule 35, before it was amended, authorized federal district courts to "correct an illegal sentence at any time." According to the Supreme Court in the *Morgan*[70] and *Hill*[71] cases, this provision was narrower than it looked: The only sentences that could be attacked under Rule 35 were those not authorized by the judgment of conviction. That is to say, the petitioner could not attack the conviction itself; he could argue only that, assuming the conviction was valid, the sentence had been unlawfully imposed. Thus Rule 35 provided no relief for such matters as illegal searches or coerced confessions; and as appellate review of sentences was expanded in conjunction with the promulgation of sentencing guidelines, Rule 35 was cut back still further.

A second collateral remedy occasionally employed to review criminal convictions is the writ of error coram nobis under the All Writs Act, 28 U.S.C. § 1651, which empowers federal courts to issue writs "necessary or appropriate in aid of their respective jurisdictions." The Supreme Court upheld the use of this writ to test a criminal

---

[70]United States v. Morgan, 346 U.S. 502 (1954).

[71]Hill v. United States, 368 U.S. 424 (1962).

conviction in the *Morgan* case (supra) over dissents arguing among other things that § 2255's post-conviction remedy was exclusive and that the writ was not ancillary to the exercise of jurisdiction, as § 1651 required, since the criminal proceeding was over.

The reason the petitioner had to resort to coram nobis in *Morgan* was that traditional post-conviction remedies were apparently unavailable. Because Morgan attacked not his sentence but his conviction, Rule 35 did not apply. Neither did § 2255; for although he challenged a federal conviction, he was not in federal custody. He was in state prison, but it was not clear that he could get habeas corpus either; for he objected not to his state-court conviction but to an earlier federal judgment on which the state court had relied in enhancing the sentence for his state crime.

In short, the field of post-conviction remedies is both complex and confused and calls out for comprehensive congressional reappraisal. The problem is also highly politicized, however, especially when it comes to review of state supreme courts by federal district judges; the reader is advised not to hold her breath.